HOMEWORK WITH IMPACT

This book reveals the types of homework activity that are most beneficial to pupils' attainment and makes practical sense of the research on homework and how it can be used most effectively. Suggesting ways in which the impact of homework can be improved, this book offers practical ideas, strategies and activities that teachers can implement, trial and adopt in their own classrooms.

Linking current evidence from cognitive psychology on retrieval practice, spacing and interleaving to the setting of homework, the book includes the following:

- suggestions for effective preparation tasks
- a discussion on metacognition and how this can help pupils revise and complete school-work independently
- an overview of how we can effectively check homework
- the importance of feedback
- how schools can support pupils and parents with homework as well as the importance of having a crystal-clear homework policy.

This is essential reading for all teachers and school leaders wanting to ensure that their homework activities have a real impact on pupils' learning.

Andrew B. Jones is Assistant Headteacher for CPD and Professional Mentoring at The Reach Free School in Rickmansworth, Hertfordshire, and a Founding Fellow of The Chartered College of Teaching.

HOMEWORK WITH IMPACT

Why What You Set and How You Set It Matters

Andrew B. Jones

Routledge
Taylor & Francis Group

LONDON AND NEW YORK

First published 2022
by Routledge
2 Park Square, Milton Park, Abingdon, Oxon OX14 4RN, UK

and by Routledge
605 Third Avenue, New York, NY 10158

Routledge is an imprint of the Taylor & Francis Group, an informa business.

British Library Cataloguing-in-Publication Data
A catalogue record for this book is available from the British Library.

Library of Congress Cataloging-in-Publication Data
Names: Jones, Andrew B., author.
Title: Homework with impact : why what you set and how you set it matters / Andrew B. Jones.
Description: First Edition. | New York : Routledge, 2021. | Includes bibliographical references and index. | Identifiers: LCCN 2021006762 | ISBN 9780367637439 (Hardback) | ISBN 9780367637446 (Paperback) | ISBN 9781003120513 (eBook)
Subjects: LCSH: Homework.
Classification: LCC LB1048 .J66 2021 | DDC 371.30281–dc23
LC record available at https://lccn.loc.gov/2021006762

ISBN: 978-0-367-63743-9 (hbk)
ISBN: 978-0-367-63744-6 (pbk)
ISBN: 978-1-003-12051-3 (ebk)

Typeset in Interstate
by SPi Technologies India Pvt Ltd (Straive)

To Anand, for encouraging me to write this book, and Kunyee, for allowing me to do so.

CONTENTS

TABLES

FIGURES

PRACTITIONER RESEARCH BOXES

BOXES

ACKNOWLEDGEMENTS

I would like to start by thanking my Challenge Partners colleagues who participated in the joint research project that led to the writing of this book, especially Mike Garvey, Laura Curtis and Joe Carey; the work of all of them is mentioned in the pages that follow. I am grateful to the 'teacher researchers' at The Reach Free School who contributed ideas to the various practitioner research projects completed at the school over the last five years, including Martyn Essery, Kellie Paterson, Chris Dixon, Michael Shippey, Oliver Lukeman, Priya Patel, Faye Caldwell, Faizah Awan, Ralph Addy, Megan Gillan, Matt Sutton and Sam Robinson.

I would like to thank not only my colleagues directly involved in practitioner research but also Rachel Brindley, David Ingledew, David Weston, Professor Dame Alison Peacock, Adam Baker and Richard Booth for their reflections on homework and best practice, which are highlighted in various chapters. It is important to note that their views do not necessarily reflect the arguments made in this book. I am grateful to Carla Da Silva, Anthony Smith, Hannah Driscoll, Lucy Wickins, Dr. Sue Brindley and Dr. Ed Wickins for their constructive criticism of the text as well as Andy Noble for his advice on which classroom-based examples of best practice to use. I appreciate the numerous opportunities given to me by Challenge Partners and the Herts & Bucks Challenge Partners' Hub in both presenting and disseminating the research that resulted in this book. I would like to thank Claire Keilty and her colleagues at Cranborne Primary School for sharing their thoughts on homework with me as well as Cheadle Hulme High School for letting me use their homework policy. I am thankful to Laura McInerney and Teacher Tapp for sending out the various questions on homework used in my own research to their legions of tappers and for allowing me to use the results as part of my work.

Lastly, I would like to thank Annamarie Kino and Molly Selby at Routledge for their support in writing this book.

1 Why homework matters

Chapter overview

This chapter will briefly consider the debate around homework before introducing the central argument of this book: that homework can positively *impact* learning and achievement, especially if certain types of task are set. More in-depth analysis of the issues touched upon here follow in the later chapters but this introduction will outline the *genesis* and *exegesis* of the collaborative research project that resulted in the writing of this book.

When I was young I hated homework. Most of my detentions at school were for not bothering to do it. At home I spent more time staring at the ceiling and daydreaming than looking at my school books. I would readily lie to my parents about the amount of homework set and whether I had completed it, answering that I had when in fact I had not even attempted it. I remember going through my excuses for non-completion on the bus going to school as well as trying to complete what was set immediately before the lesson in which the homework was due. My excuses ranged from family events preventing me from completing it to leaving it in my bag, which I had conveniently left on the bus. If I were to ask my teenage self about homework, I, like many other children, would have demanded its abolishment – arguing that it was a waste of time, a chore and an infliction I didn't need.[1]

It is ironic that I am now on the other side of the homework divide. I take no prisoners when homework is not completed, readily giving out sanctions for its absence or for an insufficient amount done. I will call parents if pupils persist in failing to hand it in and I put them on report as a further reminder that it needs to be done no matter what. Despite my former homework-dodging antics, I am now firmly of the opinion that homework has its place in the greater scheme of learning and that it is vital to pupils' success at school. A number of things have led to my change of mind, including action research, the views of my colleagues and pupils, and reflections on my practice. I am convinced that homework matters and that teachers should set it regularly. However, I also believe that some homework tasks are *more impactful* than others. Subsequently, this book makes a case for homework, especially how it *should be set* to maximise impact on learning and achievement.

The debate around homework

The impact of homework, which can be defined as any school work set and completed out of school hours or instructional time (Cooper, 1989a; Bembenutty, 2011), on learning and achievement continues to be a source of controversy amongst pupils, parents, senior leaders and governors. There are also major differences of opinion amongst classroom teachers on whether we should be setting homework as well as how much and how often. Many of my colleagues have debated these issues, studied them as part of master's courses or simply formed their views after years of setting homework and battling those who, like my former self, are reluctant to put pen to paper anywhere outside of the classroom.[2] Many are pro homework and believe it not only helps pupils learn but also instils good learning habits (see the 'arguments for' in Table 1.1). Others feel that homework is more useful at Key Stage 4 (upper secondary), especially as part of revision or preparation for future lessons, but are more ambivalent on its uses at Key Stage 3 (lower secondary) and at primary level. A minority are against homework altogether and state that they set it as part of school policy but feel it has limited impact on learning as a whole. (Some of the reasons for this are listed in 'arguments against' column in Table 1.1.)

Even though the vast majority acknowledge its benefits, teachers clearly are not unanimous on the effectiveness of homework. This is partly because there is a dearth of guidance on homework for teachers. As teacher-led studies of homework have found out, a vast amount of academic research on the role and value of homework has been published, which in turn has led to significant media interest, but this research is not written for teachers

Table 1.1 Common arguments for and against homework[3]

Arguments for homework	Arguments against homework
• Helps consolidate learning	• Tasks are often too long
• Allows practice of skills	• Tasks are often poorly devised
• Allows knowledge retrieval	• The school day is long enough
• Allows pupils to prepare for future lessons	• Homework is set for the sake of it
• Allows pupils to prepare or revise for important assessments or exams	• Pupils may copy each other's homework
• Allows pupils to further research the subjects and topics they are interested in	• Parents may help pupils complete tasks
• Builds independent learning skills	• Some parents can help their children whilst others find it difficult
• Develops other skills, such as self-regulation and good organisation	• Some parents cannot afford the best equipment and/or resources to help their children
• Makes use of resources outside of school, such as libraries	• Causes arguments between children and parents
• Gives parents an opportunity to see what their children are learning	• Takes away opportunities to rest and play
• Gives parents an opportunity to help their children	• Prevents children from taking part in activities outside of school, including sports clubs
• Allows home–school communication	

(Waters et al., 2013). Research on the impact of homework has tended to be published in academic papers littered with equations, standard deviations and coefficients that not every classroom practitioner has been trained to understand. Considering also that research often focuses on particular year groups, subject areas, ability groups or demographics, we can arguably assume that most academic studies are relative to the researchers' sample groups. However, despite acknowledging these issues, this book will argue that homework is an essential strategy for improving learning and raising achievement and will do so by *combining ideas* from academic research with practitioner action research and my own experiences of setting, marking and giving feedback on homework. Moreover, the book resulted from concern amongst local senior leaders that our homework practice could be improved and, in particular, be evidence-informed (see Box 1.1).

The impact of homework on learning and achievement

Importantly, many academic studies have shown that homework *does* impact learning and achievement. Although this statement is a generalisation, it is a central justification for not giving up on the idea of homework – despite some of the concerns listed in Table 1.1. For example, Cooper and colleagues (1989a, 1989b, 2001, 2006, 2007), amongst others, have conducted a series of major meta-analyses on the impact of homework, which have shown that the correlation between test scores and homework is *generally positive*. More recent studies, including those by Fan, Xu, Cai, Ile and Fan (2017) and Daş, Şentürk and Ciğerci (2017), have also identified positive correlations between homework and achievement in various subjects and contexts; some of these studies will be explored in more depth in Chapter 2 and should not be ignored by teachers, parents or even pupils with strong views on homework.

Similarly, studies by the Department for Education (DfE) have shown how homework can impact pupils' overall attainment. For instance, DfE researchers have noted the *strong*

Box 1.1

Reflections on homework from Rachel Brindley, Trust Improvement Director at the Danes Educational Trust

As part of the strategic meeting of collaborative senior leaders from various schools that decided to explore homework as a joint research project, Rachel states,

> The definition of Homework is, in itself, a tricky one. In relatively recent times, it has morphed from the fairly secure if uninspiring model of "Read and copy out p. 5 of the textbook." (which implicitly made all sorts of assumptions about the recipient) to, in the best practice: learning beyond the classroom that is relevant and sharply focused; that both draws on past curriculum coverage and facilitates thinking about what is to come; that provides opportunities for exploration and active practice; that receives specific and timely feedback and, probably most importantly, is pitched appropriately.

This thinking is reflected in the later chapters of this book.

evidence that pupils who reported spending 2 to 3 hours doing homework on a typical school night, compared with those who did not, attained higher grades on average (Sammons et al., 2014). Moreover, year 9 pupils who reported spending between 2 and 3 hours on homework on a typical weeknight, compared with pupils who did not spend any time on homework, were almost 10 times more likely to achieve 5 A*-C (now 4+) grades (ibid.). It is clear, then, that homework is not to be dismissed as an irrelevant or meaningless ritual hanging over us from a bygone age of redundant attitudes to teaching and learning.

Nevertheless, many teachers investigating homework as part of action research projects, like those discussed below, or as part of academic courses have suggested that the most inconclusive aspect of research on homework is what types of assignments, tasks or activities are most impactful on learning. *Yes, homework can benefit, in fact does benefit, learning and achievement, but how do we make sure that what we set maximises the impact of homework on pupil outcomes?* Critics of homework will also point out that any of the perceived benefits highlighted in research on homework show only a *small impact* on learning and achievement, but this ignores the fact that homework is not always *set in a way* that benefits learners.

The purpose of this book, therefore, is to address this issue. If we are to defend the use of homework, then it is imperative that we identify *what types of homework work best* as well as prove that the *benefits of homework outweigh the negatives*.

The genesis of this book: Challenge Partners and CamStar research

This book is the result of a series of teacher-led research projects completed on the relevance and impact of homework, which was the focus of the Herts & Bucks Challenge Partners' Hub joint research project for the 2017/18 academic year (see Practitioner Research Box 1.1). The Hub is a grouping of like-minded schools committed to improving pupil outcomes by sharing best practice. It is part of the wider Challenge Partners network that extends to over 480 schools across the UK.[4] We used existing expertise within the Hub, including the knowledge and wisdom of our many colleagues who met in discussion groups and working parties across a range of schools, to help facilitate the research process that also included knowledge and guidance from the University of Cambridge's CamStar (Cambridge, School Teachers and Research) programme; this is a network of schools that work together to support school-based teacher research.[5]

It was clear from initial discussions that the age-old issues around homework, not least how the burden of workload can be managed whilst maintaining the best pupil outcomes, remain areas worthy of investigation. Importantly, the project was inspired by the need to understand homework in our own contexts, particularly working towards a greater under-standing of how the type of homework tasks we set impacts on our pupils' achievement. Nevertheless, I feel that our experiences and findings are of use to others; hence this book.

Towards an exegesis of the research: why the type of homework you set matters

By mid-autumn 2018, the working group involved with the project at The Reach Free School (TRFS) had already agreed that homework is generally beneficial. We knew this from the

Practitioner Research Box 1.1
Action research projects

Throughout this book, you will come across a number of 'Practitioner research' boxes. These boxes contain the findings from various research projects, including those directly linked to the Herts & Bucks Challenge Partners' Hub/CamStar joint research projects on homework and retrieval practice. The boxes also contain some indirectly linked National Professional Qualifications in Middle Leadership projects as well as research from HertsCam, which is an organisation similar to CamStar aimed at building a network of teacher researchers (see www.hertscam.org.uk).

Essentially, all of these pieces of research can be seen as *action research*. This means that the research is carried out by practitioners in the field of study – in this case, teachers in schools as opposed to researchers based outside of schools. These studies are small-scale and contextual but important in the sense that they allow us to trial, measure and evaluate the ideas or strategies that we are implementing within our own classrooms or settings.

It is hoped that the inclusion of these projects will contextualise the wider academic studies discussed in this book. Also, please feel free to conduct projects similar to those cited here. One of the ideas of action research is that it is cyclical in nature – in that practitioners will need to constantly reflect on and review the strategies implemented from their findings. This might result in further research to tweak, readjust or change the ideas or strategies used and can also be carried out by other interested colleagues in differing contexts.

gargantuan meta-analyses briefly mentioned above, the DfE's own research and various other studies, such as the Education Endowment Foundation's (EEF's) *Teaching and Learning Toolkit* reports on homework at both primary and secondary levels (EEF, 2020a, 2020b). However, as stated already, we were also aware that most of the research indicating the positive benefits of homework does not question the impact of different types of homework tasks on learning and achievement. Here, research by Darling-Hammond and Ifill-Lynch (2006) suggests that teachers should set homework but also make it purposeful and relevant, which suggests that some types of homework tasks will be better than others.

Subsequently, we wanted to unearth which types of homework tasks have the most impact on pupil progress and outcomes, especially as this would help us decide which types of homework to regularly set our own pupils. Here, writers on homework tend to identify at least four types of generalised learning activity as common homework tasks (see, for example, Rosário et al., 2015; Dobozy, 2010; Cooper, 2007):

- practice homework, which involves questions, exercises or tasks that directly relate to content that has already been taught
- preparation homework, which involves preparing for an upcoming lesson. This could involve pre-reading or looking over new material prior to studying with the teacher.

- traditional revision, which would constitute the re-reading of materials and notes from lessons
- extension/extended homework, which could include longer homework activities, such as investigating the causes of World War I, writing book reviews or creating newspaper articles.

When the working group at TRFS discussed the above types, they suggested that we include two other types:

- creative homework, which could include building motte-and-bailey castles in history or making mobiles of the solar system in science
- finishing-off homework, which is the straightforward completion of unfinished work from the lesson.

These latter two were included because, after much debate, it was quite clear that we set these types of homework tasks regularly in some subjects, especially at Key Stage 3. Various discussions on each of these types of task and their impact are the basis for Chapter 3 of this book and have led me to propose that certain types of homework task, namely practice- and preparation-based homework tasks, are more relevant and impactful than others (see Chapters 4, 5 and 6). Consequently, the rest of this book – as outlined below – argues that homework not only is relevant to improved learning and achievement but can be more meaningful, purposeful and impactful if particular tasks are set as homework tasks. Therefore, the book includes considerable discussion on how homework can link to the current trends in teaching and learning best practice, specifically retrieval practice, spacing and interleaving. Not only is there plenty of evidence available to demonstrate the impact of these techniques in the classroom, but there is increasing evidence that they need to be intertwined with how we plan, set and assess homework.

Of course, other important elements of homework are considered too. These include the amount of homework to set, how to incorporate homework into curriculum planning, and parental engagement. Hopefully, this book will help you make the most of homework and *maximise the impact* it has on your pupils' learning.

Scope of this book

This book consists of 10 chapters. They cover a host of ideas that are needed to maximise the impact of homework. Chapter 2 looks at the academic research on the impact of homework. Chapter 3 looks at various types of homework and why some types are more impactful than others. Chapter 4 looks at how homework is affected by our increasingly knowledge-based curriculum and how retrieval practice is vital to helping pupils remember this knowledge. Chapter 5 examines the role of preparation homework tasks in aiding learning, takes a critical view of flipped learning and discusses independent learning. Chapter 6 gives an overview of checking learning, assessment and, importantly, feedback in relation to homework. Chapter 7 centres on planning as well as how homework can relate to current thinking on spaced distribution and interleaving. Chapter 8 looks at how we can support pupils and parents with homework. Chapter 9 focuses on writing a homework policy based on the optimal types of homework tasks. Finally, Chapter 10 summarises all of the above.

Lastly, it is worth pointing out that as an apathetic teenager who did his best to avoid homework, I left secondary school with only two General Certificates of Secondary Education (GCSEs). It was only after repeating all my exams at a further education college that I understood the impact that hard work outside of school had on my learning. It was my attitude towards homework when at school that was the problem, not the homework I was required to do.

Notes

1 These reflections were first expressed in an article I wrote for the *TES* in March 2019 on the Herts & Bucks Challenge Partners' Hub research project. Much of this book builds upon the ideas discussed in that article; see www.tes.com/magazine/article/convince-me-homework-worth-doing [accessed 14 May 2020].
2 My colleagues' opinions formed part of the Herts & Bucks Challenge Partners' Hub project, which involved a number of teacher surveys and focus groups that used both quantitative and qualitative research methods to better understand teachers' perceptions of homework (see Practitioner research box 3.1 in Chapter 3). The findings are also analysed in various blogs and papers on the project's website (see www.homeworkresearchproject.wordpress.com) as well as summarised – in part – in Appendices 2 and 3.
3 These points are all evident in the responses from teachers, parents and pupils surveyed as part of the Herts & Bucks Challenge Partners' Hub research project (referenced above) but also reflect similar points by Cowan and Hallam (1999) and Hallam and Rogers (2018).
4 For more information on Challenge Partners, see www.challengepartners.org.
5 For more on CamStar, see www.camstar.org.uk as well as www.educ.cam.ac.uk/research/programmes/camtalk/camtalkstory/.

Suggested further reading

Hallam, S. (2006b). *Homework: Its Uses and Abuses*. London: Institute of Education, University of London.
To get you started on your homework journey, read Professor Susan Hallam's outline of homework research. It is a 10-page document that can easily be found as a PDF on the internet if you put the title in a search engine. It essentially summarises arguments for and against homework, gives an overview of the research up until 2006 and also discusses studies on the attitudes of parents and others. It is well worth a read. A lengthier study was published in 2018 (see Hallam & Rogers, 2018).
EEF (2020). *Educational Endowment Fund Teaching and Learning Toolkit (Primary and Secondary Homework sections)*. London: EEF.
The EEF's guidance on teaching and learning offers a comprehensive overview of research and current thinking on homework. It has a primary and secondary section. If you are starting to research homework, it offers a good starting point; otherwise, it offers a summary of what you really need to know.

2 What does the research say?

Chapter overview

This chapter offers an exposition of the research on homework, including the gargantuan meta-analyses looking at the impact of homework on pupil *achievement*. It will also consider the differences between primary and secondary schools in relation to homework and achievement and whether there is an *optimal amount* of time for spending on homework.

When the Herts & Bucks Challenge Partners' Hub decided to research homework in the 2018/19 academic year, a colleague of mine working at another local school quipped that the project 'sounds like a headache'. He went on to explain that he had decided to research homework for a Master of Arts in Education thesis but – as suggested in the previous chapter – was completely bamboozled by the academic gobbledegook of the research and utterly confused by what people were trying to say. He eventually decided to focus on another area of teaching and learning.

He was right. There is a huge amount of academic research on the purpose, impact and value of homework and a lot of it is focused on specific subjects or phases of education that make generalisations difficult. Some academic papers look at modern foreign languages whereas others analyse only mathematics. However, what cannot be ignored is that the *vast majority* of meta-analyses and literature reviews that survey the *research as a whole* show that homework does have a *positive impact* on achievement, albeit a small one. Despite differences between primary and secondary schools, ability groups and demographic groups, I will argue that this small *positive relationship* with achievement means that homework cannot be ignored by teachers. This chapter will explore some of the key issues in 'homework research' in order to justify the argument in the rest of the book: that homework with impact can improve pupils' achievement and, subsequently, life chances. Of course, as suggested in Box 2.1, if our practice is to be evidence-informed, we must take note of academic developments in academic research.

> **Box 2.1**
>
> **Reflections on educational research from David Ingledew, Senior Lecturer in Education at the University of Hertfordshire**
>
> David believes that learning from research is an essential part of professional development. He suggests that '[r]eading and engaging with educational research and professional literature, sharing and discussing this with colleagues and peers, and reflecting upon its implications for learning and teaching, is essential for the development of the critically reflective practitioner. It deepens and enriches practice, enabling the teacher to address the complexities that they face in their own classrooms through an ongoing process of professional dialogue'. This would apply to homework as much as any other area of teaching and learning.

Mammoth meta-analyses

Most of the big research studies reviewing the overall impact of homework on learning and achievement take the form of a meta-analysis. A meta-analysis is a quantitative approach to reviewing research literature on a specific subject, such as homework. In the case of homework, a meta-analysis will typically review a number of previously published studies that directly or indirectly address whether homework impacts learning and achievement. The reviewed studies are usually conducted by a number of different researchers in a variety of educational contexts. By expanding the amount of data to include varying contexts, an improved quantitative estimate can be made of how much a given strategy impacts pupils' learning. It also makes for stronger *generalisations* as the sample sizes are increased and the research becomes more representative.

Importantly, most widely cited meta-analyses show that homework does impact learning and achievement; the vast majority suggest that homework has a 'modest' or 'moderate' *effect size* or impact, which can be clearly seen in Table 2.1. (Box 2.2 includes a brief guide to effect sizes, and a fuller explanation of effect sizes and *correlation coefficients* is given in Appendix 1.) From this basis, we can safely assume that improvements in setting, marking and feeding back on homework – as discussed in later chapters – could increase these 'modest' effects (or effect sizes) to increasingly 'strong' effects (or effect sizes) over time. Some of the key studies used to justify the positive link between homework and achievement are explored below, although many others show that homework has a generally positive impact on learning (see, for example, Graue, Weinstein & Walberg, 1983; Paschal, Weinstein & Walberg, 1984; Walberg, 1999; Fan, Xu, Cai, He & Fan, 2017; Baş, Şentürk and Ciğerci (2017)).[1]

Harris Cooper: the 'positive and statistically significant' impact of homework

Pick up any book or journal article discussing homework and it will probably mention the work of Harris Cooper. This is because Cooper and his colleagues (1989a, 1989b, 2001, 2006, 2007) have conducted a number of major meta-analyses on the impact of homework, which

Table 2.1 An overview of major meta-analyses of homework research

Synthesis study	Focus	Number of studies reviewed	Average standard deviation or correlation	Generalised level of impact*
Graue, Weinstein & Walberg, (1983)	General effects of homework	29	*d.* = 0.50	Modest impact
Paschal, Weinstein & Walberg, (1984)	Homework versus no homework	15	*d.* = 0.36	Modest impact
	Homework that is graded or has teacher comments	15	*d.* = 0.80	Moderate impact
Cooper, (1989a)	Homework versus no homework	20	*d.* = 0.21	Modest impact
Cooper, (1989b)	Time spent on homework and achievement in middle school	50	*r.* = 0.07	Weak impact
	As above, but in high school	50	*r.* = 0.25	Modest impact
Hattie, (1992); Fraser, Walberg, Welch & Hattie, (1987)	General effects of homework	110	*d.* = 0.43	Modest impact
Walberg, (1999)	With teacher comments	2	*d.* = 0.88	Moderate impact
	Graded	5	*d.* = 0.78	Moderate impact
Cooper, Robinson & Patall, (2006)	Homework versus no homework	6	*d.* = 0.60	Moderate impact
Hattie, (2009)	General effects of homework	161	*d.* = 0.29	Modest impact
Fan, Xu, Cai, He & Fan, (2017)	Homework and achievement in maths and science; completion	11	*r.* = 0.59	Moderate impact (0.01 away from strong impact)
	As above, grade	5	*r.* = 0.52	Moderate impact
	As above, effort	4	*r.* = 0.31	Modest impact
	As above, frequency	5	*r.* = 0.12	Weak impact
	As above, time spent on homework	29	*r.* = 0.15	Weak impact
Baş, Şentürk & Ciğerci, (2017).	Overall impact of homework	11	*d.* = 0.23	Modest impact
	Impact of homework in science	3	*r.* = 0.66	Strong impact
	As above, Chemistry	2	*r.* = 0.81	Very strong impact
	As above, mathematics	5	*r.* = −0.08	No impact
	As above, grade 1 to 4	4	*r.* = 0.21	Modest impact
	As above, grades 5 to 8	4	*r.* = 0.41	Moderate impact
	As above, grades 9+	2	*r.* = 0.48	Moderate impact
	As above, elementary level	7	*r.* = 0.15	Weak impact
	As above, high school level	2	*r.* = 0.48	Moderate impact
	As above, higher education	2	*r.* = 0.45	Moderate impact

Please note that the wording for the generalised impact is my own. These are adapted from the gener- alised 'effectiveness' of effect sizes estimated in Cohen (1992) and Cohen, Manion and Morrison (2007). The terminology does not necessarily reflect the views of the original researchers. Some effect sizes have been rounded off. The initial idea of this table came after I saw a similar one in Marzano and Pickering (2007).

Box 2.2

A rough guide to the impact of effect sizes

- *d.* = 0–0.20 (weak impact)
- *d.* = 0.21–0.50 (modest impact)
- *d.* = 0.51–1.00 (moderate impact)
- *d.* = 1.00+ (strong impact)

Adapted from Cohen (1992).

---

have included studies dating back to 1897. In his first synthesis, Cooper (1989a, 1989b) reviewed 20 studies that were conducted between 1962 and 1986 to see whether there was a difference in achievement between those pupils who did homework and those who did not; to help compare this, 14 studies had produced effects favouring homework whereas six favoured no homework. Interestingly, these studies showed that the typical high (secondary) school pupil completing homework outperformed 69% of the pupils completing no homework, as measured by standardised tests or grades. It is important to note, however, that this *significantly positive* impact largely relates to high (secondary) school pupils and not elementary (primary) pupils. Despite this, a more positive take on primary homework is discussed below.

A far more recent meta-analysis led by Cooper found a mean effect size of *d.* = 0.6, which suggests that homework has a moderate impact on achievement (Cooper, Robinson & Patall, 2006). In this later study, the standardised mean difference on assessments between pupils who did homework *vis-à-vis* those who did not deviated from *d.* = 0.39 to *d.* = 0.97; thus, the overall mean effect size is *d.* = 0.6. This led the researchers to state, 'With only rare exception, the relationship between the amount of homework students do and their achievement outcomes was found to be *positive and statistically significant*' (ibid., 2006, my italics).

Tom Sherrington's analysis of John Hattie's work: homework 'has an excellent effect'

As already stated above, anyone researching homework will inevitably come across Cooper and his meta-analyses. In the same way, anyone researching any area of education will probably stumble across Hattie's (2009) meta-analyses of almost everything educational. It is worth noting, therefore, that Hattie includes homework in his huge synthesis of meta-analyses. Although detractors of homework often jump on the *d.* = 0.29 effect size he gives it overall, they tend to ignore the more nuanced analysis across age groups. In *Visible Learning: A Synthesis Based on Over 800 Meta-Analyses Related to Achievement*, Hattie reaches the *d.* = 0.29 effect size after reviewing five meta-analyses covering 161 studies and more than 100,000 pupils. Nevertheless, as Sherrington (2012) points out, 'This is the best typical effect size across all the studies'. Breaking down Hattie's analysis further, Sherrington observes that the *d.* = 0.29 suggests the following:

- homework still improves the rate of learning by at least 15% (potentially advancing children's learning by about a year on average)

- that 65% of effect sizes in the analysis were positive
- that 35% of effect sizes in the analysis were negative
- but that average achievement of those assigned homework exceeded 62% of those who were not.

Again, as Sherrington points out, the *d.* = 0.29 effect size translates into a 21% chance that homework will impact achievement, which equates to 21 homework assignments set out of a 100 having any impact on pupils. Despite this 'modest impact', dig a bit deeper and Hattie calculates that the effect sizes are *d.* = 0.15 for primary school pupils and *d.* = 0.64 for secondary school pupils, which suggests much more impact than the weaker *d.*= 0.29. This effect size also corresponds to Cooper's earlier findings discussed above, which also found that homework was more impactful at the secondary level. As Sherrington exclaims, 'On this basis, homework for secondary students has an "excellent effect"' (ibid.). It is worth noting that prior to the publication of *Visible Learning*, Hattie had collaborated with other research-ers, including some of those cited above, to look at the impact of educational strategies and interventions on achievement, including homework. In a previous study, Hattie and col-leagues had suggested that the effect size of homework on achievement was *d.* = 0.43 in an analysis of 110 studies (Fraser et al., 1987; Hattie, 1992, cited in Marzano & Pickering, 2007). As an overall estimate of the impact of homework on achievement, this is somewhat more modest than Sherrington's claim that it has an 'excellent effect' but – to be fair to Sherrington – is arguably overridden by Hattie's more recent meta-analyses.

Overall, these meta-analyses go some way towards justifying the existence (and arguably importance) of homework as an invaluable intervention in our classrooms, or rather, as an extension of our classrooms. Yes, it should be acknowledged that these are generalisations and that there are concerns with the methodologies used to produce them (see Box 2.3 below). Nonetheless, as hinted at above, if the general impact of homework on learning and achievement is modest or moderate, then surely we have a duty to investigate, trial and identify *best practice* in setting, marking and feeding back on homework in order to make it a more robust, impactful and ultimately a worthwhile component of our teaching toolbox. Hopefully, the later chapters of this book will help with this endeavour.

Box 2.3

Issues with researching homework

It would be wrong to assume that the research being used to defend the use of home-work, especially the meta-analyses discussed in this chapter, has absolutely no flaws. This is openly acknowledged by researchers such as Cooper (2007). Similarly, Hallam and Rogers (2018) argue that questions should be asked of the methodology used in many of the studies that they and others reviewed. Some writers, such as Kohn (2006), have even written books challenging the research of academics like Cooper.

Indeed, Vatterott (2009) suggests that six key methodological trends in researching homework stand out, which should make us approach any findings with caution:

- Many studies rely on self-reporting, which may skewer respondent rates.
- Cumulative time spent on homework is often measured by the week and not the day.
- Sample sizes are often small and may not be representative enough to make adequate generalisations.
- In many studies, pupils are not randomly assigned to groups.
- Quite often, studies lack equivalent control groups.
- Lots of studies measure the amount of homework assigned as opposed to homework completed.

Moreover, Vatterott takes aim at researchers 'biased' by a 'familiar picture of traditional views of education' (ibid., p. 58), specifically because a lot of research focuses on:

- time as opposed to task, which suggests that many researchers believe that more time learning impacts on progress and is seemingly productive
- groups as opposed to individuals, which reflects a failure of researchers to reflect on individual differences
- pupil behaviour as opposed to teacher behaviour, which indicates a belief that the problem of poor achievement lies with the pupils themselves and not the teachers.

In a similar vein, Trautwein and Köller (2003) and Buell (2004) argue that a fundamental issue in researching homework is that pupils, classes and subjects are not uniform across time and space and that the impact of homework would depend on the expectations and experiences of different groups.

Nevertheless, despite all the concerns listed above, most analyses and reviews have demonstrated that, overall, there is a positive relationship between homework and achievement, particularly in secondary schools. These overviews pull together hundreds of specific studies carried out in various countries. The issue with all of this, however, is that the *impact is slight*, which is why – after this chapter – this book will focus more narrowly on which types of homework have the most impact on learning and achievement.

Other issues arising from research on homework

In addition to considering the meta-analyses discussed above, we should consider some less quantitative studies on the overall impact of homework. Various British academics have put together compendiums of homework research as well as detailed analyses of their own studies. One such study of note is MacBeath and Turner's (1990) *Learning Out of School: Homework, Policy and Practice*, which was commissioned by the Scottish Education Department and examined homework issues and practices by surveying teachers, pupils and parents in 13 schools in different parts of Scotland. MacBeath and Turner found that – by and large – pupils, parents and teachers have a common belief in the *value of homework*. The authors also suggested that:

- many teachers, pupils and parents see the aim of homework as review or reinforcement of classroom learning
- homework should be manageable for pupils
- homework should be challenging but not too difficult
- homework should follow a pattern in terms of frequency (that pupils understand)
- pupils should understand the purpose of homework
- discussions on the purpose and goals of homework should be carried out by teachers, parents and pupils.

The significance of this study can be found in frequent references by other researchers and writers on homework, including Hallam and Rogers (2018) and Czerniawski and Kidd (2013). If you are interested in taking your own studies further, this report is well worth reading. Also, some of their suggestions are picked up in later chapters of this book. For instance, reinforcement is covered via retrieval practice in Chapter 4; making homework challenging is mentioned in Chapters 4, 6 and 7 in relation to desirable difficulties, low-stakes testing and interleaving; frequency is related to retrieval and planning in Chapters 4 and 7 respectively; and the importance of pupils understanding the purpose of homework crops up regularly.

Homework: a 'best evidence approach'

Sharpe, Keys and Benefield (2001) also conducted a significant study of homework using a 'best evidence approach', which draws on a wide range of evidence, including meta-analyses, surveys, field experiments and case studies, to formulate summaries on homework research. Their review – called simply *Homework: A Review of Recent Research* – covered 101 studies related to homework, including roughly 40% from the US, 37% from the UK and 16% from other countries. Although this review included many of the meta-analyses discussed previously, it included other studies and reached its conclusions differently. Importantly, in a vein similar to the meta-analyses, Sharpe, Keys and Benefield found that there is a *positive relationship* between homework and achievement at secondary school, particularly for older secondary pupils but not really for primary pupils or low achievers. Their literature review also included more studies from the UK, especially England, than those conducted in the US; these included Tymms and Fitz-Gibbon's (1992) survey of 3,000 secondary school A-level pupils and Holmes and Croll's (1989) study on how homework impacted the General Certificate of Secondary Education (GCSE) results of grammar school pupils. Both of these found homework to have a *positive*, albeit marginal, impact on achievement; again, bearing in mind my argument above, we could improve upon this marginal impact if we base our homework practices on evidence-informed ideas, especially those currently being championed by cognitive psychologists and scientists (see the next chapter).

The review by Sharpe, Keys and Benefield was one of the first studies I stumbled across when attempting to make sense of the research on homework and, although it is out of date, one of the findings in the summary had a massive impact on the direction of my own thinking and the evolution of the Herts & Bucks Challenge Partners' Hub research project; the authors made clear that '[t]here is insufficient definitive research into the impact of different types of assignment… [as well as] different approaches to marking and feedback' (Sharpe, Keys and Benefield, 2001, p. iii, 27). I do my best to answer this, including using some further research, in the next chapter.

A more recent review of the research evidence

Other excellent sources of knowledge on all things homework can be found in reviews by Cowan and Hallam (1999), Hallam (2006) and Hallam and Rogers (2018). The 2018 review of homework in *Homework: The Evidence* finds the relationship between homework and achievement to be complex, especially as there are lots of challenges in researching homework. Although Hallam and Rogers argue that much of this research is of poor quality, they still find that homework has a *small positive impact on achievement* overall. Like the meta-analyses discussed earlier, their review sees this impact to be more beneficial in secondary schools than primary schools. Their other key findings related to achievement include the following: having prior knowledge and skills puts pupils at an advantage when completing homework, whereas pupils who have less knowledge and skills take longer to complete homework; parental aspirations count more than parental interference; and it is important for pupils to be able to manage homework workload and have a healthy attitude towards completing homework. Like Walberg (1999) and Cooper (2007), Hallam and Rogers found that feedback can improve the impact of homework on achievement. These issues are included throughout this book: prior knowledge in relation to retrieval practice (Chapter 4), parental engagement (Chapter 8), workload (Chapter 7), and the importance of feedback (Chapter 6).

Importantly, for British readers, Hallam and Rogers feel that there is a dearth of research on homework in the UK, which raises problems for educators as the Office for Standards in Education, Children's Services and Skills (Ofsted) (2019) has stopped giving guidance on homework. This, coupled with educational reform placing more emphasis on knowledge and curriculum coverage, means that many teachers and school leaders might feel lost at sea when it comes to following guidance on homework policy.

Accounting for differences between lower- and higher-year groups (or primary and secondary school pupils)

It is clear from all of the reviews and studies discussed so far that homework tends to have less impact in primary (or elementary) than secondary (or high) school. However, various studies unpack this a bit more. For example, Cooper and Valentine (2001) and Cooper (2007) suggest the following:

- Younger pupils find it harder to stay focused and are distracted easily.
- Younger pupils do not have the independent study skills or habits conducive to completing homework, whereas older pupils do.
- Homework is set differently and serves different purposes at primary and secondary levels. Essentially, the aim of homework is often different at primary level, where, for instance, younger pupils may be set homework centred on skills that are not assessed.

- Homework set for lower-ability pupils in lower years takes longer to complete (often because they will complete the tasks whereas older pupils will spend far less time on them or bypass compilation altogether). This means that time spent on homework will have a negative effect size or correlation in lower-year groups.

However, despite the seemingly weak impact of homework on achievement in lower-year groups, Cooper (1989b) still recommended homework for elementary (primary) pupils because a lot of learning takes place beyond the classroom and pupils must develop good homework study habits for their future school years. Furthermore, Cooper, Robinson and Patall (2006) identified a number of studies at grades 2, 3 and 4 (years 3, 4 and 5 in the UK) demonstrating that homework can have a positive impact, even if these studies were in the minority. This has led Cooper to suggest that homework is still relevant to younger pupils as it can encourage positive attitudes, habits, and character traits and reinforce the learning of basic skills taught in class. As pupils progress through the years – to upper elementary grades in the US or Key Stage 2 in the UK – homework should start to play a more direct role in academic practice and, subsequently, achievement. Lastly, in the sixth grade (Key Stage 3) and beyond, it should play an important role supporting pupils' preparation for standardised tests or public examinations (also see Marzano & Pickering, 2007).

Importantly, in relation to the above, I try to reference primary homework tasks as much as secondary (Chapters 4–9). Some of the ideas advocated in these chapters have been suggested by primary teachers who feel that, if set properly, homework does impact primary pupils. See, in particular, the section on interleaving in Chapter 7.

Time spent on homework: the 10-minute rule

So, how long should pupils spend on their homework if it is to have any impact? In the US, the National Education Association and the Parent Teacher Association recommend the *10-minute rule* for determining how much homework to set pupils (Blazer, 2009). This rule is a general guideline that suggests 10 minutes of homework per grade level (or year group) per night. For instance, this could work out at 30 minutes per day for year 4 pupils and 120 minutes per day for year 11. Various studies back this up, even if the idea is contested (see, for example, McPherson, 2005; Shellard & Turner, 2004). The idea of a 10-minute rule is supported by some of the studies we have already seen. For instance, Cooper (1989a, 1989b) found that up to 1 to 2 hours of homework a night impacted on achievement outcomes for junior high school pupils but that achievement then decreased the longer pupils spent doing their homework. Cooper, Robinson and Patall (2006) found similar findings. In their analysis, 7 to 12 hours of homework per week produced the largest effect size for 12th-grade (year 13) pupils, which means that the optimum amount of homework for impact might be between 1.5 and 2.5 hours per night (see Marzano & Pickering, 2007 as well).

Curvilinear considerations

Subsequently, there is evidence that the relationship between time spent on homework and academic achievement may be *curvilinear*, which means that homework may have a greater impact on pupil achievement when teachers set moderate amounts of homework as opposed to too little or too much (Blazer, 2009; McPherson, 2005; Sharp, Keys & Benefield, 2001). For example, Lam (1996; cited in Blazer 2009) used National Education Longitudinal Study data in the US to compare the amount of time spent on homework with the achievement test scores of over 8,000 12th-grade (year 13) pupils. Although pupils who said they completed homework had better achievement outcomes than those who did not, the most impactful relationship between homework and achievement was found amongst pupils who reported doing 7 to 12 hours of homework per week. Pupils who reported doing over 20 hours a week had test scores similar to those of pupils doing between 1 and 6 hours of homework per week. These findings are echoed in studies analysing Trends in International Mathematics and Science Study (TIMSS) data by Keys et al. (1997) and Mikk (2006).

If, then, the *optimal amount of time* spent on homework is roughly 2.5 hours per night, does this mean we have a magic number on which to base homework tasks? Here, any answer would be muddled by other factors impacting on homework. For example, individual pupils need more time to complete homework tasks, partly because of ability and interest but also because of varying time management skills (Suarez et al., 2016; Hallam & Rogers, 2018). Additionally, a 2013 study of 4,317 pupils from 10 high-performing high schools in the US found that serious mental and physical health problems occurred amongst pupils doing too much homework (Galloway et al., 2013). These included higher stress levels and sleep deprivation (see Practitioner Research Box 2.1 as well). It is worth noting that pupils, especially after a busy day at school, have limits on how much information they can take in before 'the brain needs downtime and time to process information' (Jenson, 2000, cited in Vatterott, 2009, p. 63). Of course, any claim to an optimal amount of time for completing homework will also be impacted by the absence of a quiet space at home, an overall lack of resources, and limited access to computers or broadband connectivity and parental support (OECD, 2014).

Practitioner Research Box 2.1
Megan Gillan – Research on how long pupils spend on homework and the amount of sleep they get

Megan carried out some research for the Herts & Bucks Challenge Partners' Hub homework project on how much time The Reach Free School pupils spend on homework as well as how much sleep they get. For Megan, although a lack of sleep might not be directly related to homework, it could be relevant if pupils are spending excessive amounts of time on their set tasks.

Year 11 responses showed considerable variation between those completing no homework (9%) and those saying that they spent over 3.5 hours doing homework (13%). Thirty-four per cent of pupils responded that they spent around 2 or 3 hours completing homework. Similarly, year 7 pupils showed significant variance between those completing no homework (13%) and those completing between 2 and 3 hours (5%). Here, 35% estimated that they had 1 hour on average. This resulted in the school researching optimal times for homework as well as rewriting their homework policy to make homework timing explicit. Importantly, staff were given training on this during In-Service Education and Training (INSET) sessions, which also referenced wellbeing.

Megan also found that 66% of the year 7 students surveyed stated that they got less than the recommended length of sleep for an 11- to 12-year-old, which is 9 to 10 hours a night. Sixty-three per cent of year 11 students reported not getting at least 7 hours of sleep per night, which is recommended at around 9 hours per night. Of course, this is probably multifaceted, but we are acutely aware that homework could affect the sleeping patterns of our more diligent and anxious pupils. This was included in Megan's training session.

Megan delivered this research in a presentation to the research group based at The Reach Free School (TRFS). She is Second in Department for Science.

In response to this, Chapter 7 discusses how we can plan to mitigate some of the issues mentioned above and ensure that we set homework in line with an optimal amount of time for the pupils we teach. Suggestions are made on the optimal amount of time for various year groups as well as the practicalities of ensuring that pupils can manage their homework tasks, which is also addressed in Chapter 8. This is also relevant to Chapter 9, which suggests incorporating this research into homework policies.

Set homework in small chunks

Importantly, research also indicates that homework tasks should not cover vast swaths of knowledge but be *focused* on certain areas if they are to have maximum impact. For instance, studies show that pupils learn more when allowed to practise fewer skills or concepts (Healy, 1990; Marzano, 2005) and that complex processes should be broken down into *smaller chunks*, or be focused on particular skills, in order to be properly understood by pupils (Marzano et al., 2001; Marzano, 2005). Pupils in my own school also prefer homework to be set in small chunks (see Practitioner Research Box 2.2). All of these points will be expanded and explored in more depth – and in a practical sense – in Chapters 3, 4 and 7.

Practitioner Research Box 2.2
Priya Patel – Pupils' views on maths homework – unstructured interviews

Priya carried out some research for the Herts & Bucks Challenge Partners' Hub homework project at The Reach Free School (TRFS) on pupils' views of homework. These focused on her year 9 maths class and consisted of various unstructured interviews. Priya delivered her research in a presentation to the research group based at TRFS.

Overall, pupils found homework to be beneficial – or impactful – if they could focus on tasks they initially struggled with but were starting to get the hang of. Importantly, one pupil explained to Priya that these homework tasks need to be set regularly but must not be too long. Another pupil interviewed also suggested that tasks that rein-force what is learnt in lessons are also really helpful. However, a common theme was being set too much and in a 'rushed' fashion. This led to Priya emphasising the impor-tance of short and concise maths homework, focused on practice tasks, that take place every day. In turn, maths is the exception at TRFS in that it is the only subject that is set daily as opposed to weekly.

Priya is a teacher of mathematics at St. Columbus College, St. Albans, Hertfordshire.

The importance of joined-up thinking

Lastly, we need to be wary of equating time spent on homework directly with achievement. As Marzano and Pickering (2007) make clear, a significant amount of research indicates that any positive impacts of homework are often dependent on what pupils *complete* as opposed to the amount of time spent on the tasks set. Therefore, poorly planned ad-hoc homework tasks may have an adverse impact on pupil achievement (EEF, 2020a, 2020b). Another element affecting how pupils manage time to effectively complete homework is the quantity set by teachers. If this is not planned, then pupils might struggle to complete the tasks set. Here, MacBeath and Turner (1990) suggest that there are times when pupils have too much homework to cope with, often as a result of poor subject timetabling. As the authors point out, 'It is unreasonable to expect pupils themselves to resolve the problems caused by timetabling or lack of inter-departmental consultation' (ibid., p. 38). They go on to suggest that two approaches for dealing with this issue are (1) to timetable homework allocation and (2) to provide systematic guidance and support for pupils in coping with it, including giving adequate notice of homework. The importance of a planner was also high-lighted by Baker (2007), who completed a study on a school in Cromer, Norfolk. The planner not only was seen as a successful tool but was found to be appreciated by many pupils in the school. As implied above, later chapters, particularly 7, 8 and 9, will address these issues in a more practical way.

Other areas of concern

Before finishing this chapter, we should note that there is a wealth of research on specific aspects of homework not included here. For instance, studies have looked at the effect of socioeconomics, gender and ethnicity on homework and achievement as well as the home environment and parental attitudes. Whilst a few of these issues are referenced in later chap-ters, more analysis on these particular areas can be found on the Herts & Bucks Challenge Partners' Hub project blog.[2]

Key takeaways from Chapter 2

- It is evident from the mammoth meta-analyses discussed at the beginning of this chapter as well as the other studies covered throughout that homework does impact learning and achievement, especially at secondary level.
- Although this impact is small and reasons for it continue to be debated, it would be wrong of teachers to bypass homework on the assumption that it has no impact or that the evidence is not there.
- Of course, the research is muddied by the many variables and other questionable methodological issues, as outlined above, but researchers are well aware of this and generally call for far more research to be carried out on the impact of homework; this includes teachers like us researching and improving our own practice.
- It is clear that we should not set too much homework and that there is an optimal amount that should be set.
- If we take pupils' views into account here, we will need to pitch homework at the right ability level, ensure that it can be completed and that it is clearly explained; in other words, it should be 'manageable'. Making homework manageable would square getting the optimal amount of time, which is curvilinear, with the right amount of challenge in the work set; this could involve 'small chunks' of quality activities.
- The above point will inevitably involve some whole school planning by leaders and a homework policy that ensures that these issues are addressed.
- For primary schools, perhaps a greater rethink on how homework is set and managed is needed, as pupils are hampered by basic literacy and numeracy skills.
- Some of these issues are revisited in later chapters.

Essentially, the research is not perfect and there is room for improvement but that does not mean we should underestimate the impact of homework on learning and achievement.

Notes

1 These studies were reviewed as part of the Herts & Bucks Challenge Partners' Hub homework project and used in drafts of this chapter. Further analysis can be found in the blogs on the Hub's website (see www.homeworkresearchproject.wordpress.com).
2 As above. These blogs are also posted on my own blog: www.mrjoneswhiteboard.blog.

Suggested further reading

Hallam, S. and Rogers, L. (2018b). *Homework: The Evidence*. London: UCL Institute of Education Press. Anyone wanting to really understand the research on homework and get an overview of its scope should get a copy of this book. The authors' authoritative and critical review of countless studies on homework covers more than the research touched upon in this chapter, including issues such as gender, ethnicity and socioeconomics as well as in-depth analysis of studies on teachers', pupils' and parents' views on homework.

Cooper, H. (2007b). *The Battle Over Homework: Common Ground for Administrators, Teachers, and Parents* (3rd ed.). Thousand Oaks, CA: Corwin Press.
Cooper has been cited liberally in this chapter but that is because he has dominated homework research. This book pulls together his findings and thinking into one volume. Although sections of the book could be expanded considering the author's knowledge, they are a concise and useful resource for understanding the significance of Cooper's (and his colleagues') contribution to understanding the impact of homework.

3 Which types of homework tasks have the most impact?

Chapter overview

This chapter presents an argument as to why *practice* and *preparation* homework tasks are *more impactful* than other types. It includes a brief examination of the limited research on homework types, ideas from cognitive science and reference to the Herts & Bucks Challenge Partners' Hub research project. The chapter then considers the role of other types of homework – other than practice and preparation – and why, despite some positives, they are *less impactful* on learning and achievement.

As discussed in the previous chapter, academic researchers have written a lot about homework, but the literature can be quite infuriating as many researchers do not define different types of homework tasks when assessing the generalised benefits (or limitations) of homework. This section of the book, therefore, endeavours to identify and categorise some key *types* of homework tasks. Controversially, though, I will then argue that certain types of homework tasks, namely *practice* tasks and *preparation* tasks, are *more impactful* than others. Although other types of homework tasks may have their place, the case will be made that creative, collaborative and project-based tasks have limited impact on pupils' long-term learning and achievement, particularly their mastery of subject knowledge and skills. We will look at various evidence-informed and anecdotal justifications for the chapter's assertions, which build on the views of my colleagues involved in the Herts & Bucks Challenge Partners' Hub research project, 2,259 other teachers in the UK and my own pupils (see Practitioner Research Box 3.1). Therefore, I will compare and contrast practice, preparation, extension, project, creative, collaboration, revision and finishing-off tasks in order to make the case for the first two types (see Table 3.1 for brief explanations and examples).

The case for practice and preparation over other types: the research

By and large, there seems to be a slow but *emerging consensus* amongst some researchers and writers that practice and preparation homework has the most impact on developing

Practitioner Research Box 3.1
The main findings of the Herts & Bucks Challenge Partners' Hub research project on homework (2017-2018)

The Hub's homework project involved the views of teachers, pupils and parents. It included my own school, two non-selective comprehensive schools, two partially selective schools and a selective grammar school. A primary school was also involved in the later stages – this school was from outside the Hub. It is clear that the majority of colleagues canvassed for their views as well as the pupils involved in research trials found practice and preparation tasks the most impactful types of homework. Some key areas of research are listed in this box.

- **My immediate colleagues**. Sixty-nine per cent of staff at The Reach Free School involved in a homework working group, which involved 18 members of staff and lasted for one academic year, believed that – after researching and setting different types of homework in their subject areas – practice homework had the most impact on pupils' learning, progress and attainment. By contrast, creative and finishing-off homework activities were seen to have the least impact on pupils' learning, progress and attainment. Staff identified types of task and agreed on the operationalised typing, which was similar to Table 3.1.
- **Colleagues in other schools**. Studies were completed in other Hub schools, and the consensus amongst researchers was that practice and preparation tasks were more impactful than other types of homework. For example, see 'Practitioner Research Box 5.1' and the work of Laura Curtis (Chapter 5). Similarly, 80% of teachers (from a sample of 20) at a local primary school suggested that practice homework tasks are most beneficial at Key Stages 1 and 2.
- **Pupils**. In a survey of 50 pupils, 74% said they felt that practice-based homework activities had improved their assessment grades the most. The pupils were asked to complete different types of homework and then qualitatively assess which improved their knowledge, confidence and exam skills. They did, however, use their assessed work to make this albeit subjective judgement.
- **Two control groups**. These groups showed that 91% and 92% of pupils were on target at the end of the trial period (where they were set only practice homework activities) as opposed to 45% and 79% respectively prior to the trial period (where homework activities were mixed).
- **Teacher Tapp**. Over 2,259 teachers took part in a quick survey, based on the questions we asked our pupils and staff, which was sent out by Teacher Tapp (an app for teachers that 'buzzes' them with questions each day at 3:30 p.m.). These results, I feel, corroborate the results from pupils and staff in my own setting. Most (62%) teachers thought that setting homework activities centred on practising something already taught in class 'best help' pupil outcomes (although they could tick more than one option).

The outlier here was parents where only 14% saw practice as the most impactful type. Here, 25% chose creative and 25% chose none at all. This survey had 64 respondents. Nevertheless, in relation to my reliance on teachers' views, it can be argued that teacher perspectives are essential to understanding homework as we are the ones who design, set and assess homework tasks (Epstein & Van Voorhis, 2001).

Of course, the project was limited geographically and involved input from only one primary school, but it did allow the participants to explore the impact of different homework tasks in their contexts. A fuller examination of my own involvement with the project can be found in Appendices 2 and 3. Additionally, further analysis can be found on the project's website: www.homeworkresearchproject.wordpress.com.

Table 3.1 Types of commonly set homework tasks[1]

Type of homework task	Explanation	Examples
Practice	Questions, exercises or tasks that directly relate to content that has already been taught.	General Certificate of Secondary Education (GCSE) or A level–style questions, past papers, previously taught skills, low-stakes tests recalling key subject knowledge etc. at secondary or letter formation, number bond practice, times tables etc. at primary.
Preparation	Preparing for an upcoming lesson or series of lessons.	Reading set texts before an English lesson, learning vocabulary prior to using it in French lessons etc.
Extension	Longer homework assignments that get pupils to research new content independently and in-depth, learn new ideas by themselves or combine both the latter activities in extended projects.	Investigating the various causes of World War I over an extended period, writing book reviews (non-curricular), creating newspaper articles on issues of interest, a termly project on the Romans, possibly going to places of interest etc.
Revision	The re-study of completed work in preparation of an assessment or exam.	Traditional revision techniques include re-reading notes, re-reading tests, taking additional notes etc.
Creative	Tasks that involve making things, especially those that involve art and imagination.	Making mobiles of plant cells in science, making medieval shields in history, making posters on Islam in religious education etc.
Collaborative	Tasks that involve pupils working together in pairs or groups.	Presentations, joint research projects, the performance of role plays, group problem solving etc.
Finishing-off homework	The completion of work not finished in class.	Finishing off incomplete notes, colouring in, textbook questions that were not finished etc.

pupils' cognitive, or rather academic, ability (Cooper, 2007; Hallam, 2006; Hallam & Rogers, 2018; Edwards, 2017). Many agree that homework should generally be about reinforcing what pupils learned in lessons, which is particularly true of linear acquisition subjects such maths, science and languages but also essential to the retention and application of subject knowledge in all other curriculum subjects (see Practitioner Research Box 3.1, for example).

For instance, although Cooper (1989a, 1989b) found that practice and preparation tasks had a limited impact on pupils' attitudes to homework, their impact on immediate and delayed achievement measures was more evident. Here, pupils who included practice and preparation tasks alongside other tasks outperformed their peers by 54% (figure cited in Hallam & Rogers, 2018). Eighteen years later, Cooper also suggested, 'distributing the content of homework assignments so that it includes material meant to practise past lessons or prepare for future lessons, or both, is more effective than assignments that include only same day content' (2007, Chapter 3, Section 2, Paragraph 9). This means homework that involves activities that extend learning beyond the content taught in the lesson have less impact than practise of previously taught content or preparation tasks, especially if those activities are distributed over time. Similarly, Hallam states that there is 'evidence that, on both immediate and delayed achievement measures, homework which includes preparation, practice or both is more effective than homework concerned only with current curriculum content' (2006, p. 3).

Practice, if set properly, arguably makes perfect

Following on from the above points, Marzano, Pickering and Pollock (2001) argue that when homework is set for the purpose of practice, it is best to structure the tasks around previously taught knowledge and skills that the pupils are already *familiar* with. For instance, if pupils are asked to practise a skill they learnt in a previous lesson for homework, they need to be taught that skill *beforehand*. Essentially, practising a skill with which the pupil is not familiar will cause misconceptions and errors that could well be repeated. This will also be the case with the application of subject knowledge; if pupils need to outline, explain, analyse or evaluate a question that tests their knowledge, they will need to be taught both the skills and the knowledge needed for a credible answer prior to attempting. Research also suggests that the speed and accuracy of pupils' responses to questions will improve if practice tasks are *regularly* set; these are key indicators of the effectiveness of homework as well as progress over time (ibid.). Importantly, practice tasks give pupils multiple opportunities to practise content that has been previously taught in class, which will lay the foundations for new learning. By setting frequent homework tasks that centre on practising the application of subject knowledge or skills acquired in class, teachers can provide pupils with a greater chance of developing *fluency* with the subject knowledge and skills taught (Pickering, 2003). Lastly, it is important that the pupils be aware of this. According to Marzano (2017), practice homework is even more impactful if pupils 'summarize what they have learned from the homework and reflect on their level of effort' (p. 60; see Box 3.1 as well).

Box 3.1

Reflections on homework from David Weston, CEO of the Teacher Development Trust

When asked about what the potential benefits of homework are, David said '[to] practise, consolidate and extend learning from lessons and to prepare for the next lesson or to produce something for discussion and feedback'. He then suggested that '[i]t also builds study habits and encourages more time for thinking and reflection about the subjects/topics [studied in school]'. It is important to note that David uses the words 'learning from' and 'reflection', which underscore the importance of building and reflecting on what has been learnt in class.

Be prepared

Moving on from the above focus on practice homework, Marzano (2017) also suggests that pupils should be given homework to *preview* new content or *prepare* them for new learning; however, it is important to stress that this still needs to be planned and guided if it is to have any impact. For instance, Lee and Pruitt (1979) argue that a common issue with preparation homework is a lack of clear instructions. An absence of clear instructions means that pupils may learn the wrong content or become confused by the information presented. Moreover, the purpose of the task, including its role in the subsequent lessons, might not be understood. Lee and Pruitt also point out that any preparation homework should be immediately evaluated or followed up in the next lesson; like many researchers writing today, they advocate low-stakes testing, particularly quizzes, as a method to do this. In relation to this, Epstein and Van Voorhis argue that *well-designed* preparation homework can 'stimulate students' thinking about a topic, for example, when teachers ask pupils to outline ideas for an essay that will be written in class' (Epstein & Van Voorhis, 2001, p. 182). Therefore, so long as preparation homework is planned by teachers, it can be 'given to prepare students to *gain maximum benefit* from subsequent lessons' (Lee & Pruitt, 1979, p. 32; italics added). Lastly, Bujis and Admiraal conclude that the strategy of preparing analytical homework tasks can increase pupils' time on task and their class participation in later lessons, making it an '*effective*' homework task (2013, p. 777; my italics).

Cognitive science and evidence-informed best practice

In the absence of additional studies on types of homework, it may be worth going beyond research focused on homework and briefly looking at the current trends in *evidence-informed* best practice. An increasing body of knowledge champions the importance of retrieval practice, spaced distribution and interleaving (see, for example, Karpicke, 2012; Carpenter & Agarwal, 2019; Bjork & Bjork, 2011). These ideas will be explored in the next chapters and, in a similar vein to Marzano, Pickering and Pollock (2001) above, emphasise the importance of *practice* and *rehearsal* of previously taught knowledge. Of course, it is worth pointing out that some researchers and writers question the extensive use of these strategies as homework tasks (see Box 3.2).

Box 3.2

Arguments against practice homework tasks

Not everyone agrees that practice makes perfect in terms of homework, especially if practice tasks become drill-like exercises. For instance, developmental psychologist Ellen Langer has argued that, '[w]hen we drill ourselves in a certain skill so that it becomes second nature', we may come to perform that skill 'mindlessly' (cited in Kohn, 2012, p. 111). Here, some researchers suggest that practice homework tasks can be harmful to those who do not understand what they are doing or who have learning difficulties. As DeVries and Kohlberg (1990) state, 'Such homework makes them feel stupid and can make them accustomed to doing things the wrong way (because what's really "reinforced" are mistaken assumptions)' (cited in Kohn, 2012, p. 113).

Another issue that could dampen the impact of practice-based homework tasks is that motivation and interest are important factors in relation to the successful completion of homework (Trautwein & Köller, 2003; Hong et al., 2015). Pupils who are motivated and interested are more inclined to complete their homework; this could have profound effects on those who feel that practice-based homework tasks become drudgery. Arguably, practice-based homework may not inspire pupils in the way that creative or extended project work could (although there is next to no research demonstrating this).

Despite these concerns, I think that practice tasks can extend beyond pure drill and incorporate various types of activities, including puzzles and a mixture of tasks that allow more abstract thinking (see the next chapter for examples). Furthermore, if we ensure that pupils receive regular feedback on their homework, then surely mistaken assumptions can be corrected.[2]

Moreover, many researchers and writers are questioning some of the key ideas that could underpin project work, which is a common form of extension task. Christodoulou (2013), for instance, argues that the idea that projects are the best way to learn is a 'myth'. This is because expecting pupils to research, comprehend ideas and even solve problems in new areas of study is complicated by the fact that children are not experts in the first place. Moreover, for Christodoulou, the assumption that pupils can just look up information without encountering misconceptions and incorrect ideas and that twenty-first-century learning is conducive to exploratory, self-directed study is highly problematic. Furthermore, expecting pupils to use libraries, visit museums and purchase the resources often needed for project or creative homework is also problematic. It ignores, of course, issues of cultural capital, material deprivation and parental involvement in homework. This is *not* to say that these tasks should be completely jettisoned, but it is worth considering all the hindrances a pupil may encounter if there is to be any impact from these types of homework tasks.

The role of other homework types: extension tasks

Though less impactful on pupils' achievement outcomes, other homework types do have benefits if used in a purposeful way. Extension tasks that allow pupils to develop their understanding of topics taught in class in more depth out of class have an appeal, especially in terms of widening pupils' knowledge and getting them to make links between taught content and additional areas of the curriculum. Many teachers would equate these activities with Bloom's (1956) higher-order thinking skills as well as critical thinking. As Lee and Pruitt (1979) suggest, extension tasks can be given to facilitate opportunities for pupils to transfer a new skill or concept to a new situation, which echoes Bloom's taxonomy where synthesis and evaluation are deemed to be higher cognitive skills than remembering and basic understanding. Lee and Pruitt go on to say that extension homework tasks differ from practice tasks in 'the degree of application and abstract thinking required. Practice assignments require very little thinking' (ibid., p. 32). Although I *completely disagree* with the second point, if pupils are interested and engaged enough to further their learning through extension tasks, I see no reason why this may not extend their application of abstract thinking. Moreover, extension activities could make impactful 'stretch and challenge' tasks for both 'more able' pupils as well those with an interest in the subject (regardless of ability). Lee and Pruitt suggest that a good example of an extension activity could be a comparative explanation of different revolutions; if, say, the French Revolution were taught in class, then pupils could go home and compare it with the American Revolution. Perhaps British pupils could do this with comparisons of Tudor monarchs or the rise of different totalitarian governments in the 1930s. Lee and Pruitt also use the example of explaining the relationship between two human organs within class time and then asking pupils to write additional explanations of the relationships between other organs as homework.

However, this use of homework extension tasks does not fully address the issue of *misconceptions* and what to do with *more apathetic* or even some less-able pupils, who may well struggle if given limited instructions with the expectation that they will 'extend' their learning through intrinsic fascination. I would also argue that Bloom's higher-order skills can be part of practice and preparation homework tasks. For instance, an evaluative answer to a question on euthanasia in religious education requires pupils to practice their evaluative skills whereas selecting which parts of a text are most important to quote in a forthcoming English lesson demonstrates how evaluation can be part of a preparation homework task.

Nonetheless, a take on extension homework similar to that of Lee and Pruitt comes from Corno (1996). Referencing the work of Hill (1994), Corno suggests that some homework tasks can use pupils' experiences of home, which can be brought into school to enrich learning. This approach emphasises pupils' 'individual histories' to further engage them in learning. For instance, 'Hill notes that when students are encouraged by teachers to attend the events in their daily lives outside school, they have a greater involvement with school' (Corno, 1996, p. 29). To illustrate this, Hill recounts pupils catching tadpoles in a pond away from school and out of school hours before categorising them and studying them amongst themselves; this is then discussed within school with the teacher. Importantly, 'Astute teachers systematically support their students to integrate the real world with school experiences' (Hill, 1994, cited in Corno, 1996). Here, we see homework as multifaceted, as active learning can take place alongside collaborative projects that could also foster more participation in class. This type of learning is arguably less suited to straightforward practice and preparation homework tasks, but I would caution against the *assumption* that all pupils have the *opportunities* and *access* to these experiences out of school. I would also question whether modern teachers *have time* to map their pupils' hobbies and interests against their syllabi and the wider curriculum, especially if curriculum time is limited.

Project work

Many people feel that enriching the curriculum with extended learning tasks, such as project work, can allow pupils to further their interests at home. It also allows them to develop independent learning skills, hone their ability to self-regulate and engage in wider sources of learning than school-based work permits, such as using public or specialist libraries as well as visiting museums or the outside environment. Additionally, project work over time allows pupils to use their critical thinking skills, develop their communication skills, collaborate with others and be creative in their production of work. It also allows pupils to have an element of choice in what they either research or decide to include in their research as well as providing opportunities for continual feedback and revision of their work as they go along (for a discussion on choice and homework, see Practitioner Research Box 3.2). Many would also argue that project work involves plenty of problem solving, and advocates would highlight how this promotes active learning and higher-order thinking skills (Savery, 2006). Indeed, homework-based project tasks may be designed to engage pupils in active learning activities, such as conducting and reporting experiments for science homework, writing essays on topics of interest or critiquing a book, for example (see Corno, 2000; Epstein and Van Voorhis, 2001).

Practitioner Research Box 3.2
Joe Carey – How can we encourage students to genuinely enjoy learning at home?

Joe's Herts & Bucks Challenge Partners' Hub/CamStar research initially involved surveying 140 pupils and 35 teachers to gather their views on homework before choosing five 'innovative tasks' to use as case studies. Through careful analysis of what things were working for their pupils, Joe and his colleagues were able to construct basic principles for what makes a homework task engaging within their context. Furthermore, they aimed to go a step further and generate a list of adaptable tasks to enable staff to refresh their own thinking. The selected tasks built upon the ideas of Carr (2013), who suggests that the hallmarks of high-quality homework tasks are purpose, efficiency, ownership, competence and aesthetic appeal. The specific tasks trialed included the following:

- **'Surprise-me homework'**. Pupils are given a time frame and a general topic area. They must complete a piece of homework in any format of their choosing.
- **'You-choose homework'**. Pupils are asked to come up with two or three ways of proving they have consolidated their learning. The class then pick from the options.

- **'You-set-it homework'**. A different pupil is selected each lesson to design a home-work task for the rest of the class. This is then copied and distributed for the group to complete.
- **'Over-to-you homework**. Pupils are each given a different topic or section of work. They then deliver this to the class with a handout/visual aid.
- **'On-location homework'**. Pupils are given a task to complete in a specific location. They must then submit the work with a photo of where they completed it.

Contrary to other research within the Hub (see Practitioner Research Box 3.1), which largely emphasised the setting of practice and specifically structured preparation tasks, Joe's findings showed that pupils enjoyed being given autonomy and freedom when deciding what homework tasks to complete. These five homework tasks each have their own benefits – however, collectively Joe and his colleagues found that they increased pupil engagement, especially as the tasks were specifically designed to encourage pupils to carefully select and digest information for themselves. Subsequently, Joe recommends that class teachers try these tasks out on their own pupils.

Of course, this research is contextual to the school in question.

Joe is Head of Year 8 at Sir John Laws School, Harpenden, Hertfordshire.

Nonetheless, the impact that these projects have on pupils' long-term memory and – if the projects are not regularly revisited – their subsequent *impact on achievement are questionable*. As suggested earlier, plenty of evidence suggests that pupils should be taught – initially at least – in small bite-sized chunks. These steps in the learning process should be well thought out and gradual as well as allow plenty of opportunity for practice (see, for example, Rosenshine, 2012; Coe et al., 2014; Sealy, 2019). For instance, I remember spending hours with my son at the Science Museum in London learning about space exploration for a school project – it was a fantastic day out – however, when I asked him 6 months later about the differences between an astronaut and cosmonaut, he had completely forgotten. The project had been in-depth and – in terms of facilitating time together – really worthwhile, but I feel that if he were to commit this knowledge to his long-term memory, then we would need to regularly practice exercises where this knowledge was retrieved. Although I would still like my son's teachers to set these homework tasks, I am under no illusion that they will necessarily impact his progress in science. I should add that my son was lucky enough to be taken to one of the world's leading science museums – not every child is.

Creative homework tasks

Lee and Pruitt (1979) also discuss the setting of creative homework and its benefits for pupils. For instance, creative tasks could require pupils to integrate various skills, including fine motor skills, with their conceptual understandings of the work attempted. Moreover, researchers such as MacBeath and Turner (1990) have found that pupils often enjoy imaginative and creative homework tasks and that these can be a great motivator in getting them to complete their homework. Away from creative arts subjects, examples could include creating intricately illustrated timelines of historical figures in the humanities or the creation of advertising posters in business studies. Some of the most beautiful homework I have seen has included the building of medieval castles in history as well as projects on everything from superheroes to the Egyptians at primary level. The latter projects often include the building of models, illustrations and extended pieces of writing that involve extensive use of the imagination, such as diary entries.

However, despite this, issues remain. Although pupils (and adults) often have vague recollections of completing these pieces of work – indeed, some parents may hold onto them – there is a question as to whether the facts, ideas and concepts learnt are always committed to long-term memory if not revisited via practice homework tasks such as retrieval practice. Sealy (2019) refers to these memorable activities as *episodic memories*, which are highly contextual and bound together with the sensory experiences and emotions we had at the time. For instance, I recall spending hours creating a model of the Rocky Mountains with my son with wood we gathered from the local nature reserve and plenty of paint and glue. It was fun. However, in a similar way to our Science Museum visit, a few months later he remembered the model and the trip to the woods but he could not explain the ecosystem of the Rocky Mountains, which was the core learning objective of the topic. The opposite of our episodic memories are our *semantic memories*, which are context-free and largely devoid of the sensory and emotional responses found in our episodic memories; they require more frequent practise and, according to Sealy, are more adaptable as they are not linked to an autobiographical memory that can be hazy and imprecise if recalled in an exam or applied to a new learning situation. Also, creative tasks often involve resources, which could – as constantly repeated here – affect pupils from a more disadvantaged background. Yes, these homework tasks can be enriching and rewarding, but they do have *clear limitations* (see Box 3.3).

Box 3.3

Reflections on homework from Professor Dame Alison Peacock, CEO of the Chartered College of Teaching

Professor Peacock raises the importance of cultural capital and other life chances in relation to homework. She states,

> For far too many families of young children homework can become a battle ground. It can also fuel parental competition – which family can produce the most intricate working model of a Spitfire plane, create a fancy-dress costume, prepare a project file etc.? In the best scenario the home learning task is to some degree open ended and allows for individual or family response and blame is not attached to the outcomes… Home learning and life experience in the broadest sense, impacts on achievement and is probably one of the greatest determiners of future learning success. This relates to cultural capital and general knowledge gained through a wide range of experiences such as travel, conversation and debate with interested caring adults.

However, she still feels that homework has a place in children's lives if it allows them opportunities to 'practise independently what they have learnt in school or to engage in pre-learning or flipped learning'.

Collaboration

It could also be said that pupil interaction outside of school and their wider participation in school life may be enhanced by homework tasks other than practice and preparation. For example, whilst finding that pupils felt their outcomes were impacted most by practice assessments via fragmented tests, Buijs and Admiraal (2013) found that jigsaw assessments, which involved getting pupils into groups and facilitating high degrees of interdependence, yielded the highest impact in terms of time on task and class participation. Epstein and Van Voorhis (2001) similarly suggested that homework tasks may be designed to encourage pupil collaboration, which – in turn – can motivate them and allow them to learn from each other. Here, collaboration can be formal with assigned roles and expectations or informal with pupils simply chatting about how they are completing tasks. There is even evidence that collaboration on homework tasks can improve achievement in English and maths (Azmitia & Cooper, 2001, cited in Epstein & Van Voorhis, 2001). This element of homework design is arguably better placed in extension activities that allow pupils to approach the work discursively and with additional amounts of time to work together. However, one issue I have with this emerges from my own experiences of setting this type of homework task. Essentially, I agree that these activities can be rewarding and enriching, but it is *dependent on all of the pupils collaborating and pulling together* as well as the teacher either getting the grouping right or having complete faith that pupils who choose their own collaborators do so wisely. I have lost count of the times that pupils have failed to complete work because of falling out, some element not being completed by one of their members or clear evidence that someone has done most of the work for the others. Yes, use collaborative tasks if they work with your pupils and the context of your lessons, but do not rely on them.

Revision and finishing-off homework

Revision has an interesting relationship with homework and will be explored in more depth in Chapter 5. Essentially, research suggests that revising is more impactful if it entails certain techniques, such as retrieval practice strategies with self-testing or elaboration (Dunlosky, 2013; Kirby, 2015). Moreover, these specific strategies – discussed in the following chapters – are more beneficial if distributed over time and interleaved, which is essentially mixing up topics as opposed to revising them in blocks. Therefore, revision is useful for consolidating learning from the classroom through further independent application of knowledge and practise of skills. In a way, it could be argued that practice of past papers combined with a revision timetable is a good fit for impactful revision; obviously, project work is redundant at this stage and creative homework will have limited impact unless the information is part of a dual coding exercise or takes the part of a visual knowledge organiser.

Another issue with revision is how pupils are directed or taught to revise. Again, this is discussed in Chapter 5, but it is worth noting here that studies show that pupils find it hard to structure their time away from school and that self-regulation can be difficult. Indeed, we saw in the previous chapter that making homework manageable was one of the key things that teachers can do to help pupils. Therefore, it helps if pupils are taught revision strategies and are given timetables to organise themselves.

Lastly, finishing-off homework really results from a lack of pace and planning in the classroom. Although it is one of the most set homework tasks amongst teachers and often liked by pupils, its effectiveness is directly related to the activities that were taking place in the classroom. Some of those activities may have less impact at home away from the teacher – who can clarify misconceptions, correct mistakes and answer questions that otherwise would be burdensome to find – as well as other pupils if pair or group work has been facilitated. Furthermore, there is a danger that finishing-off homework is set purely because the teacher has not planned a more effective homework task in the first place.

Key takeaways from Chapter 3

- Though limited and contested, academic research tends to suggest that many types of homework tasks are ineffective and that more activities should be focused on practising knowledge recall, knowledge application and exam-style questions on content that has already been taught or finding constructive ways for pupils to prepare for future lessons.
- The Herts & Bucks Challenge Partners' Hub study concluded that practice and preparation homework tasks impact on achievement, especially at secondary level, more than other types of homework.
- Moreover, whereas the Hub research groups included the importance of preparation homework tasks in the assessment of impactful homework, my own research and experience saw practice tasks overshadow preparation tasks in terms of impact by some distance.
- Current trends in classroom best practice, especially evidence-informed teaching and learning, add weight to the argument that practice and preparation tasks have more impact on learning achievement than other types.
- Of course, there are differences of opinion here, but I feel that many academic articles suggesting that pupils partake specifically in extension, creative or collaborative tasks have been superseded by recent developments in cognitive psychology and science.
- However, that is not to say that extension, creative or collaborative tasks have no place in the greater scheme of things and these tasks can certainly be enriching. But when setting and celebrating these tasks, we must be aware of the impact of cultural capital, socioeconomics and pupils' home environments in addition to the lesser impact the tasks may have on pupil outcomes overall.

The following chapters will explore these ideas in a more practical sense and offer strategies for improving how we set, mark and give feedback on homework.

Notes

1 These types of task and examples were discussed amongst the practitioner researchers, but the typing is also informed by academic research (see, for example, Cooper, 2007; Danielson, Storm & Kramer, 2011; Rosário et al., 2015; Yu, 2015; Minke, 2017).

2 More critical analysis of academic research on homework can be found on the Herts & Bucks Hub Homework Project website: www.homeworkresearchproject.wordpress.com.

Suggested further reading

The Herts & Bucks Challenge Partners' Hub Joint Research Project on Homework. Retrieved from: www.homeworkresearchproject.wordpress.com [20 June 2020].

Various schools within the Herts & Bucks Challenge Partners' Hub completed a joint research project on improving the impact of homework throughout the 2017/18 academic year. You can explore the project's website to learn more about our findings, including what types of homework task work best. The website includes blogs, research papers and links for further reading.

Lee, J. F. & Pruitt, K. W. (1979b). 'Homework Assignments: Class Games or Teaching Tool?'. *Clearing House*, 53(1), pp. 31-35.

This article is a little dated, but it is one of the few that tackles types of homework tasks in any real depth. I include it here as many of the authors' suggestions and arguments go against the ideas expressed in this chapter. It includes discussion on practice, preparation, extension and creative homework with some evaluation of all four types.

4 Knowledge, memory and retrieval practice

Chapter overview

This chapter considers the importance of knowledge in relation to homework, especially as educational reforms over the last decade have emphasised the centrality of a *knowledge-rich* curriculum. This sets the scene for a discussion on the importance of using homework to improve pupils' *long-term memories* and their ability to *recall facts*. Combining research from cognitive science with the ideas of my colleagues, this chapter will pay particular attention to *retrieval practice* as a homework task.

There is probably not one teacher, or trainee teacher, reading this who has not had training on *retrieval practice*. The phrase – as one university lecturer put to me in an email when I offered to do some training on it – is 'somewhat trendy at present'. This is true. When I trained to teach in 1996, most of the advocated strategies revolved around the terms *active learning*, *group work* and *skills for life*. Moreover, in my first years of teaching, I sat through countless In-Service Education and Training (INSET) sessions on learning styles, building learning power and personal learning and thinking skills. On one occasion, when the A-level results of my pupils were not up to scratch, I was carted off to a training day with an educational charity that told me to be 'more of a facilitator than a teacher' in order to raise my pupils' grades via independent learning. Although some of these ideas – perhaps not learning styles – have their place, I largely ignored everything I was being told and continued teaching in a mildly didactic way with plenty of video clips for engagement, followed by regular questioning activities and topped off with lots practice questions; I have done well out of this in terms of results and honestly feel that any 'success' is due to the *way I teach* as opposed to any mighty prowess in the classroom; I still suffer from regular bouts of imposter syndrome.

Interestingly, INSET sessions and teacher training have largely changed too – hence my lecturer colleague's use of the word 'trendy'. A lot of the fashionable ideas bandied about in the late 1990s and 2000s have been either proven to be ineffective or, in some cases, completely debunked. It is here, then, that terms like *retrieval practice*, *low-stakes testing*, *spaced distribution* and *interleaving* have come to the fore. The evidence seems to be there to jus-tify their prevalence and, in this chapter, I will seek to link some of the ideas associated with retrieval practice to the setting of homework. (See Chapter 6 for low-stakes testing; spaced distribution and interleaving will be covered in Chapter 7.) There will also be a healthy dose of practical strategies tried and tested by myself or my colleagues (or both) to illustrate the points I make.[1] I should caution, however, that although I use a lot of the current teaching strat-egies being advocated by various 'trendy' experts, most of the links made to the setting and compilation of homework are made by me and do not necessarily reflect the views of the origi-nal researchers, writers or bloggers. Moreover, these direct and indirect links can be seen as part and parcel of a continuous process of learning, especially in relation to retrieval practice.

Nonetheless, before we get going, it might be worth looking at a bit of context in terms of current expectations of teachers in the UK, especially those in England and Wales follow-ing the National Curriculum, as the rise and increased emphasis of knowledge and subject-specific skills over the last decade further demonstrate the importance of retrieval practice in our teaching, including what we set for homework.

Background: the centrality of knowledge

In 2013, the then government decided that the UK's public examination system, which includes General Certificates of Secondary Education (GCSEs) and A levels in England, Wales and Northern Ireland, needed reforming after continual bombardment from the press and other critics that the system was too easy, not fit for purpose and that grade inflation was becoming increasingly evident. Although many teachers – who actually work in schools – were wary of these cynical attacks on the profession, sweeping reforms were introduced by ministers and their advisors. Subsequently, the taught content of the GCSE and A-level syllabi were made more *knowledge-based* (or, in the case of maths and science, more focused on quantitative problem-solving). As the then Secretary of State for Education, Michael Gove, stated:

> Reformed GCSEs must prioritise stretching assessment, which truly tests the depth and breadth of pupils' knowledge and abilities... Internal assessment and the use of exam aids should be kept to a minimum and used only where there is a compelling case to do so, to provide for effective and deep assessment of the specified curriculum content.
>
> (Gove, 2013)

For example, the reformed GCSE in English literature is now completely 'closed-book', mean-ing that pupils cannot take the texts they have been preparing for into the exam. Unlike in the 'open-book' exams of the past, pupils' reliance on memory and their ability to recall – or retrieve – key quotes or narrative is arguably harder than when they could dip into a text and check their understanding or find a relevant quote. Although necessary extracts from the texts are still provided within the exam paper, there is greater emphasis on the requirement to criti-cally compare and contrast a range of literature from memory (Howard & Khan, 2019). This means that pupils have to recall key information in addition to applying the relevant skills to unpack, analyse and evaluate those texts, which is arguably more challenging without the texts in front of you. These reforms were not limited to secondary level, however, as changes to the National Curriculum impacted on primary schools as well. Greater consideration of facts and figures features here; this included understanding events in chronological order in history (Hodkinson and Smith, 2018) as well as understanding grammatical rules in English and the terminology associated with them (Watson, 2018). Here, the reforms place greater awareness on form-focused approaches to grammar as opposed to meaning-orientated approaches. This upped the complexity of teaching grammatical terminology to such an extent that teachers had to attend training on what it all meant (Dean, 2016).

Clearly, Gove and his colleagues put knowledge at the centre of these reforms. He even stated, 'Our new curriculum affirms – at every point – the critical importance of knowledge acquisition' (Coughlan, 2013). Other examples included the following: teaching 'early memorisation of tables, written methods of long division and calculations with fractions' in maths; emphasising 'the scientific principles and laws which drive proper understanding of the natural world' in science; the 'proper locational knowledge with an understanding of how to use maps and locate rivers and oceans, cities and continents' in geography; and 'a clear emphasis on the importance of translation – including the study of literature of proven merit' in foreign languages (ibid.).

This heavy focus on increased knowledge was championed by some and deplored by others, including the teaching unions. However, some researchers strongly suggest that young children are capable of grasping complex temporal concepts, such as chronology-ordering facts, so long as teachers carefully plan for their development through targeted activities (Hodkinson and Smith, 2018). Indeed, Gove himself was influenced by the writing of E.D. Hirsch, who argues that all pupils need to learn facts in a highly organised and structured way based on a curriculum of *core knowledge*. Subsequently, both Gove (SMF, 2013) and other government ministers, such as Nick Gibb (DfE, 2017), have name-checked Hirsch and other advocates for the teaching of more in-depth *subject knowledge*, such as Christodoulou (2013). It is clear, therefore, that these thinkers have impacted on what we teach in our schools and how we teach it.

So, what has this got to do with retrieval practice, let alone homework? Perhaps I can answer this by going back to Gove – a man I often feel passionately at odds with – in order to answer this. In his emphasis on the centrality of knowledge to learning, which is now reality for pupils in England and Wales, Gove cited Professor Daniel T. Willingham as one of the world's most respected cognitive scientists. Willingham (2006) believes that extensive factual knowledge underpins pupils' ability to apply other skills that are often deemed superior to mere remembering. Moreover, it is only when subject knowledge is secure in the *long-term memory*, through activities that strengthen pupils' ability to retrieve information and knowledge, that facts and figures can be successfully applied to new tasks and challenges. Here, I would completely acknowledge that Gove (or rather the experts he read) was right to suggest that our ability to think critically and to analyse and evaluate everything from interpretations of history to the proof of scientific experiments *is dependent on extensive background knowledge*. As Gove himself states, 'This accumulation of evidence – from schools, states and scientists – comes as close to being irrefutable as anything in public policy' (SMF, 2013). It is here, then, that retrieval practice comes into play. Furthermore, its relevance to homework cannot be bypassed, as one of the key justifications for homework is the acknowledgement that curriculum time is limited and that pupils need more time to practice and master subject knowledge and skills; this argument was often used before the curriculum became more focused on knowledge acquisition, but it is clearly more pertinent now that the curriculum is even more *knowledge-based*.

Long-term memory and schema

Although I do not want to get bogged down in too much psychobabble and scientific jargon (there is enough in this book already and I am no cognitive psychologist or scientist), it is worth briefly mentioning the idea of *schema* in relation to long-term memory, especially in juxtaposition to the idea of the short-term and working memories. Essentially, our short-term memory has the capacity to hold a small amount of information, which will be remembered for a short period of time; '*it does exactly as it says on the tin*'. An example of this information could include a date given in a meeting; you tend to write this information in your diary pretty quickly as you know you will forget it soon enough. Some cognitive psychologists and scientists also refer to the working memory, which can be distinguished from short-term memory, even if it is often mixed up by teachers and trainers alike. Importantly, the latter is limited to the short-term storage of information whereas the former allows for the application, manipulation and evaluation of this stored short-term information. The working memory is central to decision making but is also temporal as any immediate information we receive will be forgotten unless we return to it. Long-term memory, on the other hand, relates to the storage of information indefinitely or for an extended period. There are, of course, different theories and models of this form of memory as well as different types. Nonetheless, our concern is using homework to bridge the gap between the short-term and working memory with the long-term memory.

If we want to commit knowledge to long-term memory, then the concept of a schema (or *schemata* – plural) is helpful and will occasionally be referred to below and in the next chapters. Schemata are mental concepts that help us understand complex objects and ideas, often by categorising individual facts or concepts into larger groups of facts and concepts, which are interconnected. Didau and Rose (2016) argue that schemata allow pupils to link smaller *chunks* of information, which in abundance could overload our short-term and working memories, into larger chunks that increase their chances of committing new information to the long-term memory. Here, cognitive psychologists and scientists often talk of *encoding*, which can be seen as the way you first learn of something and can include the visual, acoustic or semantic relaying of information, for example. Subsequently, schemata affect the way knowledge is encoded and retrieved, supporting the idea that our memories are reconstructive as opposed to a state of random occurrences.

Again, what has this got to do with retrieval practice and homework? Essentially, we need to set homework tasks that allow pupils to build on the schemata developing from their work in class. Here, homework is part of a longer process of encoding information and knowledge into pupils' long-term memory, especially if they are to be able to retrieve this in exams and other aspects of life. We could see homework, in this instance, as fitting into this process of knowledge acquisition as shown in Figure 4.1: the encoding stage, the storage stage,

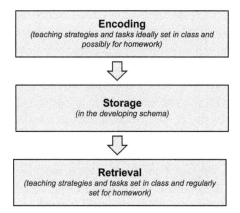

Figure 4.1 The stages of memory and their relationship to homework (adapted from McLeod, 2013)

and retrieval stage (Melton, 1963, cited in McDermott & Roediger, 2020). This is relatively straightforward as the tasks we set for homework need to consider how the information and knowledge taught are encoded and, in order to help pupils store this information and knowledge, we need to ensure that they are regularly retrieved via retrieval practice tasks. As McDermott and Roediger state, 'The central point for now is that the three stages–encoding, storage, and retrieval–affect one another, and are inextricably bound together' (ibid.).

What is retrieval practice?

Brown, Roediger and McDaniel write that retrieval practice 'not only makes memories more durable but produces knowledge that can be retrieved more readily' (2014, p. 42). Basically, retrieval practice involves pupils' recalling information from their own memories through scaffolded or learnt activities, such as making flash cards, using crosswords or concept mapping. It can include the use of low-stakes testing, such as multiple-choice questions, exam-style questions or even essays – if completed without reference to textbooks or the internet. Although many commentators link retrieval practice directly to low-stakes testing, I would include any activities that get pupils to retrieve knowledge from memory, especially those that can be set regularly for homework and allow pupils to practise recalling knowledge in a meaningful and *purposeful* way; this would include the skills of knowledge application in addition to simply recalling information. Of course, making practice purposeful involves attention, rehearsal and repetition over time as well as regular feedback (Erickson, 2008).

There is plenty of evidence to support the use of retrieval practice both in the classroom and as homework. Perhaps a good place to start is with the research by Dunlosky et al. (2013) on effective teaching strategies. Reviewing various studies, the researchers identified 10 commonly used teaching strategies that many teachers will recognise as they probably set them both as tasks in class and as homework. These were also written up by Dunlosky (2013) in his highly readable *Strengthening the Student Toolkit: Strategies to Boost Learning* (see Box 4.1). Importantly, the researchers found that *practice testing* and *distributed practice* were the most effective strategies used. This is because they can impact pupils learning, 'regardless of age, they can enhance learning and comprehension of a large range of materials, and, most important, they can boost student achievement' (Dunlosky, 2013, p. 13).

Here, the research by Dunlosky and his colleagues relates to retrieval practice in several ways. First, their recognition of practice testing as one of the most effective, or impactful, forms of learning is relevant to how we set homework. As discussed in the previous chapter, practice homework tasks impact on learning and achievement more than most other types, so setting regular practice tests or exam-style questions can be beneficial. Indeed, Dunlosky even suggested that any type of practice test, from short essays to multiple-choice questions, can have an impact on learning and achievement. In my own teaching, I often set questions or sections from past papers and, as we found in the previous chapter, the vast majority of my pupils say they find this useful. Below is an example of questions I set my pupils (Figure 4.2). Importantly, I give them separate sheets with enough lines to write on to avoid writing too much or too little (although handwriting plays a factor here). For instance, the 5 mark question in Figure 4.2 should take pupils no more than 5 minutes, which would be the case in an actual exam. An element of trust is needed here, as well as with the examples used elsewhere in this chapter, as pupils should complete the question without referring to their notes, texts or revision materials.

Second, Dunlosky also suggested that pupils should be encouraged to take notes in class but then use these notes constructively as a tool for retrieval practice. One way to do this is for pupils to re-read the notes, which is not a great learning strategy in and of itself, but then

---

Box 4.1

The review by Dunlosky et al. (2013) of the ranked efficacy of 10 popular learning strategies

1. Practice testing – taking practice tests or self-testing
2. Distributed practice – planned practice over time
3. Interleaved practice – planned practice over time that mixes the topics and subtopics so that they do not follow the order in which they were originally or logically taught
4. Elaborative interrogation – explaining why a fact or concept is true
5. Self-explanation – explaining the processes of solving a problem or how concepts are linked
6. Re-reading – going over the same text or content
7. Highlighting and underlining – picking out key pieces of information whilst reading, usually in a text
8. Summarisation – writing summaries of longer texts or pieces of information
9. Key word mnemonics – verbal association or mental images of key information
10. Imagery – visualising mental images of key information text or ideas

Adapted from Dunlosky et al. (2013) and Dunlosky (2013).

04. Explain two religious teachings on cohabitation (5 marks). Refer to sacred texts or scripture in your answers.

_____

_____

_____

_____

_____

_____

_____

_____

_____

Figure 4.2 An example of a simple exam question set for homework

cover the notes and recap the information. Here, they could bullet-point or summarise what they remember; although the latter, again, is not a fantastic strategy *per se*, it does have impact if the summarising forms part of the retrieval process. Of course, the retrieval will be more difficult, but arguably more beneficial, the longer the pupil waits before bullet-pointing or summarising. Indeed, the best strategy here might be to start by writing down what they can remember before re-reading their original notes to see how much was recalled. Although this strategy is easily identified as a practice task, it also works as a method of preparation as pupils can apply the strategy in the run-up to class assessments, standardised tests or public examinations.

Third, Dunlosky suggests that flash cards are a fantastic way to facilitate retrieval practice. I am sure that we all know what flash cards are; however, a simple description of them equates – almost – to a description of retrieval practice. For example, each card has a question on one side, which the pupil endeavours to answer by retrieving the correct knowledge from their memory, before flipping over to check whether they recalled the information correctly. In relation to homework, flash cards can be made in class and used at home, either as a direct practice task or as self-regulated revision. They can even be made at home as part of a set task to bring to the next lesson; this would constitute a preparation task. Moreover, flash cards can be used to retrieve almost anything: foreign vocabulary, quotes, historical dates, mathematical formulas or any other useful facts, figures or concepts studied.

Variance of retrieval practice activities

In addition to the three strategies discussed above, it might be worth setting different types of retrieval tasks from time to time. Most of the research on *variance*, *context* and *transfer* focuses on teaching pupils in different environments (or rooms) as well as how pupils' learning and achievement are affected by emotional cues. There are also plenty of studies on how the context of social interactions and subject domains influences what we remember – in the sense that if you learn with one group or in one subject area, it is not easy to transfer the knowledge and skills learnt to another working group or subject area. Nonetheless, there is also some evidence that varying tasks or problems can aid learning and allow pupils to actively apply the schemata in their long-term memory. Bjork (1994) suggests that a certain amount of variability in activities and tasks is both desirable and impactful on learning and achievement, which can be seen as a *desirable difficulty* (see Box 4.2). Although I regularly set past papers and certain types of exam questions, there is a mild danger that retrieval of certain facts or concepts could become contextualised to particular types of question or associated with specific units of learning; this is important as some of the facts or concepts may appear in other types of questions or in other units of learning.

Therefore, at The Reach Free School (TRFS), we advocate varying retrieval practice tasks both in the classroom and as homework so long as they are evidence-informed. The activities listed below can be set as standalone directed homework tasks or as parts of wider homework activities (in combination with other tasks). Importantly, these tasks include a number of ideas advocated by Dunlosky et al. as 'very effective' but also build upon some of the less effective ones by *making them into* practice or preparation activities.

Box 4.2

Desirable difficulties

A desirable difficulty is a learning task that is not particularly easy and requires a *desirable amount of effort* to complete or solve. This effort, in turn, has been found to improve long-term memory and performance (Bjork, 1994; Bjork & Bjork 2011). However, compared with other teaching methods or strategies, desirable difficulties can initially slow learning down and seem counterproductive. Schmidt and Bjork (1992) caution that easier tasks may well indicate immediate or temporary improvements in learning and achievement, but these should not be confused with more permanent or long-term effects. Bjork and Bjork (2011) suggest that desirable difficulties can include the following:

- varying the conditions of practice (discussed in one aspect here)
- spacing practice sessions or study (discussed in Chapter 7)
- interleaving (discussed in Chapter 7)
- generation effects (discussed below)
- using tests (discussed in Chapter 6)

It is worth noting that a lot of discussion around varying conditions of practice focuses on environment or the physical parameters of practice; however, Bjork does suggest that 'increasing the variety, types and range of exercises' has an effect on learning too (Bjork, 1994, p. 190).

Paraphrase. Pupils can put quotes, statements, definitions or relatively straightforward concepts given out by teachers into their own words; if this is a practice task, they should be prompted simply to recall the information taught in lessons; if this is set as a preparation task, pupils can read information or text and rewrite the information in a simplified form ready to use in the lesson.

Read → Cover → Copy. As it 'says on the tin', pupils read over something previously taught or soon to be taught and then cover it up or put it away; this allows pupils to see how much they can remember – word for word or as exact definitions. 'Read → Cover → Copy' can be seen as either a practice task or even a preparation task, especially if pupils are required to use the knowledge remembered in future lessons. Importantly, if set as a practice task, the copy aspect could also involve some analytic or evaluative response in order to merge knowledge and skills in the act of recall, but this might need to be modelled in class or explicitly directed by the teacher when set as a homework task.

Questions. Pupils can make a list of questions about the topic they are studying or revising, which they can use later. This – again – could be set as a practice homework task if pupils later retrieve the information from memory as part of the homework, which could be set in stages, or as a preparation homework task for a future lesson activity. Pupils could also be required to quiz each other, but this may be affected by a lack of cooperation between pupils or poor pairing and groups.

Elaborate. Pupils could retrieve information from memory and make a mind map linking the ideas and key words from what they are learning to other ideas and concepts in that subject; this is called a concept map. However, as stated above, if part of a retrieval practice activity, the information must be recalled (of course, pupils could simply elaborate by writing what they know about facts, concepts or ideas). The activity could be set as a standalone task in preparation of later work or as a prelude to a practice task.

Reflect → Write. On a blank sheet of paper, pupils write how much they can remember about a given topic. They can try to link ideas and concepts together and then check their work with appropriate resources or later in class to see how accurate they were. Of course, if set as a practice task, the reflection can be organised as an exam-style response where particular analytical or evaluative skills are applied.

Mnemonics. Pupils make memorable phrases to help remember key information (for instance, ROYGBIV – red, orange, yellow, green, blue, indigo, violet – for the colours of the rainbow). Mnemonics can be used as an aide for retrieval practice or as a preparation task prior for a soon-to-be taught lesson or test.

Revision clocks. Pupils simply draw a clock in the centre of a piece of paper or page of a book, draw lines coming out of the clock (as many as desired) and then recall the information they are learning or revising (this should, of course, be done without notes). Pupils write or elaborate what they are recalling in the relevant section; importantly, they must time themselves on each section – hence, the reference to the clock is not just pictorial (see Jones, 2019, for further discussion; Jones credits Becky Russell [@ teachgeogblog] with this idea).

Thinking quilts. Pupils are given a grid with key words or concepts (or both) and they must recall the meaning of these and add small explanations or definitions in the grid. However, they must then encode – perhaps through the use of highlighters – key categories within the subject, such as time periods in history or grouping key words into subunit areas of study; here, the activity links key concepts within a specific subject through knowledge retrieval (see, for example, Karen Knight's ideas – @KNNTeachLearn). See Practitioner Research Box 4.1 for a discussion on how this strategy and 'revision clocks' can impact attainment.

Cryptic crosswords. These get pupils to both interpret and analyse the meaning of the questions by making connections between the cryptic clue and the subject knowledge being alluded to, which is a specific key word or term that goes in the squares assigned to that clue. For an example of a cryptic crossword, see the crossword below that explores the key terms and concepts about euthanasia in religious education. This task is part of a two-part homework. The cryptic crossword gets pupils to recall key terms and concepts before tackling this evaluative for-and-against proposition: 'Euthanasia is incompatible with religious belief' (12 marks), which is based on a past GCSE paper. The crossword should take, on average, 10–15 minutes and the evaluative '12 marker' should take 12–13 minutes (Figure 4.3).

Practitioner Research Box 4.1
Oliver Lukeman – Impacting history learning via retrieval practice

The purpose behind Ollie's research and departmental improvement project on retrieval practice was to enhance pupils' retention and recall of historical knowledge at Key Stage 4, which would also help boost pupils' performance at GCSE. Ollie completed this as part of the Challenge Partners' Hub research project on retrieval practice, which followed the initial homework project, as well as for his National Professional Qualification in Middle Leadership. Ollie focused on the principles and processes of retrieving information from memory (using a variety of academic research) when trialing and implementing retrieval-based strategies and resources in his classes and those of colleagues. Many of these were used in combination with practice and preparation homework tasks. He also analysed and tracked pupils' performance data to measure the impact of the implemented strategies, which included 'thinking quilts', 'revision clocks' and 'battleships'.

Ollie says that after these retrieval tasks are implemented and evaluated, it is evident that they had a resounding impact on pupil attainment in the year they were implemented. The results of the participating year group's assessment data showed a +0.54 improvement in the average Progress 8 score year on year during the implementation period. Importantly, there was an improvement in raw data in the final mock, which had a Progress 8 score of +1.41 compared with previous years.

Ollie is now Head of History at Al Salam Community School, Dubai.

Euthanasia

Across
1. A Swiss house where passing on is permissible.
4. Let nature take its course.
7. People helping those ask for the end (two words).
10. A good death in ancient Greece.
11. This life champions general wellbeing above the divine.
12. A place of comfort and care before death.
13. An individual's choice.

Down
2. When there is no way of knowing.
3. A country where euthanasia is legal.
5. The involvement of human action.
6. Care that optimises the quality of life for those who are near the end of their life or in great pain.
8. Against their wishes.
9. The active ending of life goes against this.

Figure 4.3 A cryptic crossword puzzle used in religious education

Low-stakes testing. Pupils can complete quiz questions, especially multiple-choice questions, on paper or online. For instance, questions or quizzes can be set through popular online websites and apps, including Quizlet and Kahoot (featured in Chapter 6) as well as subject-specific sites, such as Times Tables Rock Stars or Spanish Express. You could also send parents questions to quiz their children on but – of course – this depends on how engaged your pupils' parents are and can be fraught with difficulty. Low-stakes testing is discussed in more depth in Chapter 6.

In addition to varying activities, we can set tasks that use multiple methods. For instance, my colleague Sam Robinson uses a strategy called *multiple representations* in his maths lessons where pupils are encouraged to use different methods to solve the same problem. Building on the ideas of Duncan (2010), Sam sets up mathematical problems that

- allow pupils to choose and apply various methods to solve the problem
- are not suggestive of the methods, so as not influence pupils
- often allow for formal written explanations, pictorial representations and practical ways of solving the question
- occasionally challenge pupils to apply methods to unseen problems.

In the example below (Figure 4.4), we see how pupils can find the highest common factor (HCF) of 18 and 30 using multiple representations, including the *ladder*, *prime factor tree* and *long division* methods. For those of you wary of maths, a common factor is a factor that is shared by two or more numbers. To find the HCF, a pupil lists all common factors of two numbers and simply selects the largest one in that list. Thus, if the factors of 18 are 1, 2, 3, 6,

Finding the HCF and LCM

Method 1	Method 2	Method 3

Figure 4.4 Using multiple representations to find the highest common factor (HCF) and lowest common multiple (LCM) of 18 and 30 (courtesy of Sam Robinson)

9 and 18 and the factors of 30 are 1, 2, 3, 5, 6, 10, 15 and 30, the highest common factor is 6. To find the lowest common multiple (LCM), a pupil lists all the multiples of each number and identifies the common multiples. Quite simply, the lowest one is the LCM. Therefore, the LCM of 18 and 30 is 90.

The next example (Figure 4.5) illustrates how pupils can practice three ways to divide a ratio by using multiple representations. Here, the pupil could use the *written method* or the *bar model method* or use *manipulatives* to divide 28 by the ratio 5:2, which is 8 by the way (as there are seven 4s in 28; so 5 of these together equal 20 and 2 equal 8). Again, pupils' ability to attempt division by ratio in exams will be aided by regularly practising these various methods. If they are taught and modelled in class, using guided practice tasks, they will become part of the pupils' methodological arsenal when solving these problems; in this sense, the regular setting of these tasks is retrieval practice as pupils will tackle the problems by applying the methods, which will form a schema in their long-term memory, to problems such as dividing by ratio. These tasks can, of course, be set for homework.

Dividing in a ratio

Share £28 in the ratio 5:2

Figure 4.5 Using multiple representations to divide a ratio (courtesy of Sam Robinson)

The generation effect

The *generation effect* refers to the idea that knowledge will be better remembered if it is generated via cues rather than simply read. Bjork (1994, n.d.) argues that tasks that get pupils to *generate words* rather than merely reading them can have a long-lasting impact on learning. He gives the example of using letter stems, such as 'fl___' for 'flower', as cues for retrieval of vocabulary or key terms. Here, you could set a number of letter stem cues for compilation as a straightforward homework task. The example below shows a homework set in GCSE physical education (Figure 4.6). Pupils not only generate the words from the word stem cue but also then have to recall the definition. The example below is limited to key words beginning with 'a'. This could be followed lesson by lesson with the rest of the alphabet before setting regular spaced and mixed (interleaved) versions of the tasks.

Section A – Health, Fitness and Games	
KEY WORD / WORDS	**DEFINITION**
Abdominals	Muscles found at the front of the stomach.
Abduction	Movement of a body part away from the midline of the body.
Adduction	Movement of a body part towards the midline of the body.
Aerobic respiration	Energy system that needs oxygen to break down glucose to provide energy in order for the body to function.
Age	The number of years someone has lived for before dying of old age or prematurely.
Agonists	The muscle that produces joint movement (a.k.a prime mover).
Air passage	The route the air takes to go from the mouth into the lungs
Alveoli	Small sacs of air that that allow for gaseous exchanges.
Anaerobic respiration	Energy system that works in the absence of oxygen.
Antagonists	The muscle that relaxes when the agonist muscle is in use.

Figure 4.6 A glossary featuring letter stems used in physical education

Another form of generation discussed by Bjork involves anagrams, which have been used for years but are an additional way of getting pupils to retrieve information from cues or hints. Of course, anagrams can gradually be mixed up – or interleaved – or be used in text for pupils to decipher. Some educators, such as Rosadi (2017), have found them to be beneficial for vocabulary acquisition, but they have uses in homework tasks that are embedding concepts through word association or contextual opposites as well. For example, in religious education, I might set a very simple homework task (always as a warm-up to another task) with these anagrams:

- Topnotmeni
- Citmsonine
- Evloenntebimo
- Ptnenmoeirs
- Trescannedtn
- Ammeninta[2]

Then I would give these instructions: 'Answer this question: "Explain two beliefs about the nature of God in Islam" (5 marks) using the words you have unscrambled'. By the way, word processors often change the first letter of the anagram to a capital letter. I tend to leave them that way as the pupils say it makes it more difficult!

You could also play with opposites:

- Ogod → lvei
- Avheen → lelh
- Amad → vee
- Dnee → flla
- Eifl → adhet
- Nsi → lavaanits[3]

Then I would give these instructions: 'Answer this question "Explain two beliefs about Original Sin in Christianity" (5 marks) using the words you have unscrambled'. In a way, this also helps scaffold the longer written parts of the homework. There is more on scaffolding below.

Rosenshine's *Principles of Instruction* and homework

Interestingly, Rosenshine's *Principles of Instruction* (2012) can also tell us something about setting homework with impact as well as how homework relates to retrieval practice. Although most teachers reading this have probably encountered Rosenshine's work, there is no harm in a recap (see Box 4.3). I do not wish to suggest that Rosenshine was writing about homework *per se*, but his principles clearly have a direct, or at the very least an indirect, relationship with homework, especially how it can be implemented via guided practice, modelling and scaffolding as well as regularly checked and reviewed. Moreover, the principles largely hinge on the idea of *practice*, which arguably denotes knowledge retrieval practice as much as the practice of skills. Rosenshine states that '[i]n the classroom, the most effective teachers in the studies of classroom instruction understood the importance of practice, and they began their lessons with a five to eight-minute review of previously covered material' (2012, p. 2). Here, reviews of previously taught content can include vocabulary, mathematical or scientific formulae, historical events as well as more abstract ideas and concepts. As advocated by Pickering (2003) in the previous chapter, continual review – including weekly and monthly reviews – can lead to fluency or – as Rosenshine puts it – *automatic recall*.

Although checking learning via *daily* or *weekly reviews* will be touched upon in Chapter 6, in terms or retrieval practice, Rosenshine suggests review material needs overlearning, 'i.e., newly acquired skills should be practiced well beyond the point of initial mastery, leading to automaticity' (ibid., p. 2). For me, this point is significant as it emphasises that homework is a continuation of this learning process. Here, practice is not merely a tool for recalling information – as many people simply see retrieval practice as doing – but also a tool for perfecting (to the best of a pupil's individual ability) the skills needed to articulate, explain, analyse and evaluate the information retrieved. It is, however, best if retrieval tasks are designed and delivered by teachers as opposed to pupils simply checking their own learning (see Practitioner Research Box 4.2).

Box 4.3

Rosenshine's *Principles of Instruction*

(My own thoughts on how they relate to homework appear in brackets.)

1. Short reviews of previous learning at the beginning of lessons *(homework can be used to prepare for these reviews, or the reviews can be used to check pupils' understanding of their homework)*
2. Introducing new content in small steps and allowing pupils to practice after each step *(homework can be used for follow-up practice)*
3. Checking understanding by asking lots of questions *(this can be applied to what the pupils did for homework)*
4. Modelling answers and solutions *(these models could be used before pupils continue to practice the modelled activities at home if lesson time is limited)*
5. Guiding pupils' practice *(perhaps prior to continuing practice at home)*
6. Checking pupils' understanding of what is taught *(various homework tasks can do or aid this)*
7. Obtaining a high success rate *(in terms of fluency and the mastering of knowledge application and skills, homework allows more practice time)*
8. Using scaffolds for challenging tasks *(there are, of course, ways to set homework with scaffolds)*
9. Requiring pupils to practice independently as well as monitoring this practice *(homework can help build independent practice skills and resilience)*
10. Weekly and monthly reviews *(again, homework can be used to prepare for these and, in some cases, facilitate these)*

Adapted from Rosenshine (2012).

Practitioner Research Box 4.2
Kellie Patterson and Chris Dixon - Checking homework via retrieval practice - why it should be teacher-led more than pupil-led

Following the research by Dunlosky et al. (2013) and Ben Newmark (2018), Kellie and Chris's research, which formed part of the Challenge Partners' Hub retrieval practice research project that followed the initial homework project, investigated opposing methods of retrieval starter activities; these, in turn, often built upon preparation and practice homework tasks. The research simply trialed retrieval starter activities with questions designed by teachers as well as those designed by pupils. The predicted positives would be that the structure and guidance provided by teacher input would allow pupils to access questions pitched at the appropriate level and covering a wide range of topics. This is opposed to pupil-made questions shared and completed by the whole class, which often can result in repetitive questions or a level of difficulty not appropriate for all.

Two mixed-ability classes were used for the investigation to provide as close to an identical sample as possible. In one class, a teacher led starter activities based on work from the first half term, which included practice and preparation homework tasks; a range of activities were presented to the pupils, allowing for adequate retrieval over each subtopic covered. In the other class, pupils came up with three questions, each one from a different subtopic covered previously as a method of retrieval.

Pre- and post-tests were put in place to test pupils' retention of knowledge.

The results – based on 10 pupils randomly selected from each class – showed that most pupils increased their percentage result from the first test in both classes. It was also the case, however, that there was a more significant increase in attainment in classes using teacher-led questioning in comparison with pupil-led questioning.

Kellie and Chris are maths teachers at TRFS, experienced teacher mentors and researchers for HertsCam (see www.hertscam.org.uk).

In some ways, this mirrors earlier research by Fitts and Posner (1967). They identified three phases of practice, which I think can be applied to retrieval practice and, especially, its relevance to homework.

- The first stage is the *cognitive stage*, which includes gathering information on what we need to do. At this point, our pupils' use of the information, such as how they apply it to an exam question, is sketchy. However, large gains are made as pupils are introduced to the knowledge or skill. It would be extremely difficult for pupils to learn a skill without receiving any prior knowledge about the skill, whether that knowledge is visual or verbal. This stage happens in the classroom prior to homework. Importantly, this links back to Rosenshine's emphasis on modelling and guiding pupils practice respectively.
- The second stage is the *associative phase*, which includes applying the knowledge and skills learned in the previous cognitive stage through practice exercises or activities. This stage could involve initial practice runs in class before gradually setting practice tasks for homework. Here, in a vein similar to Rosenshine, pupils' attempts at homework will still need plenty of guidance from their teachers and may also include scaffolding to support their attempts at the tasks set.
- Lastly, the third stage is the *autonomous phase*, which means that pupils – by and large and according to ability – have learned to carry out the application of knowledge and skills to tasks and problems with very little conscious effort; this is exactly the fluency that we discussed in the previous chapter, which can lead to the mastery of a subject. Consequently, homework tasks can include regular practice activities or preparation for practice tests in class.

If we are to see the obvious impact that retrieval practice can have on homework and achievement, it is important not to lose sight of Rosenshine's emphasis on modelling and scaffolding. Before we move on, perhaps it is worth looking at how modelling and scaffolding learning activities have a role to play prior to setting homework, in the setting of homework and in the application – if needed – of homework.

Modelling and scaffolding homework tasks

Modelling is an essential aspect of teaching and learning. At its most basic, modelling is when a teacher demonstrates how to complete a piece of work, action or approach to learning whilst pupils observe. Modelling for retrieval practice-based homework tasks will obviously occur in the classroom. This may happen once before the pupils practice the modelled activity at home; it may happen once before the pupils receive guided instructions or attempt the activity a number of times in class before continuing the practice at home; or it might include regular modelling over a sequence of lessons. Modelling could also be done remotely via video instruction that accompanies the homework task set if – of course – pupils have adequate access to the required technologies.

Importantly, educational psychologists have found that *direct instruction* strategies, which include modelling, have far more impact on learning than *facilitating* teaching methods, which were somewhat in vogue five to ten years ago; nonetheless, you could argue that direct instruction in the classroom facilitates independent study at home. Although there are times when facilitated group work or project work is relevant to the pupils' learning, there now seems to be a growing consensus that direct instruction has a more immediate impact on learning. For instance, Hattie (cited in Bromley, 2017) found that the average effect size for strategies where the teacher acted as an 'activator', including the active modelling of learning, was *d.* = 0.6 but that teaching strategies involving the teacher as a facilitator stood at *d.* = 0.17.

Hattie and Yates (2014) also emphasise the importance of – or evidence for – *worked examples*, where teachers take pupils through a step-by-step guide to solving problems, applying a skill or answering an essay question. Here, the authors state, 'The worked example effect now stands as one of the most robust findings from applied psychology research' (ibid., p. 151). This approach to modelling can obviously have a role to play in setting up homework activities, as does another recommendation from Hattie and Yates, the *completion example*. This strategy is essentially an incomplete worked example that the pupil completes; the first steps have been demonstrated by the teacher, and the pupil simply completes them. In a way, the guided first steps can be seen as a method of scaffolding as they support the pupil as they prepare to finish the next steps in the task at hand. In relation to homework, completion examples could be practised in class before being set as a non-scaffolded task to complete at home.

My colleague Faizah Awan has demonstrated how modelling can be used to set up homework tasks in INSET sessions at TRFS. First, she suggested that it is useful to share a pupil-friendly mark scheme, rubric or progress grid to scaffold the modelling, especially if you are using written text. The examples below illustrate Faizah's use of a progress grid; this grid will be explained to pupils so that they can use it to analyse the modelled answers both before the homework task and after in – what Rosenshine would call – a review activity (Figure 4.7).

Second, in class, pupils will also read a modelled exemplar answer (see Figure 4.8). Whilst reading they need to use the progress grid, check for any SPaG (spelling, punctuation and grammar) mistakes and then evaluate the strengths and weaknesses through 'what went well' and 'even better if' comments. This prevents passivity when reading and gets pupils to actively think about the text. This can be completed in class.

Third, pupils read another exemplar (see Figure 4.9). As previously, they need to use the progress grid, check for any SPaG mistakes and then evaluate the strengths and weaknesses through a 'what went well' and an 'even better if''. However, they can now compare and contrast the answers to see the difference between levels of response, such as a GCSE grade 4 or grade 6. This also allows the pupils to see how questions may be answered in various ways. In some ways, this aspect of modelling could comprise the last third of a lesson or the plenary where the taught content is re-explained through modelling in preparation for the set homework task.

Finally, pupils can attempt their own answers for homework. This is essentially a retrieval practice task as described by Dunlosky earlier. Faizah even scaffolds this for pupils so they know how to construct the answer and the expectations required to complete it well (see Figure 4.10). This process of modelling, scaffolding and then independent work is, I am sure you will agree, pretty thorough.

LO: To develop our responses to GCSE 12 mark questions.	**Practice question: Explain changes in medical knowledge during the period c.1500 – c.1700.**			
1. Write down and underline the date and title. 2. Look at the progress grid and model paragraph you have been given. 3. Circle and correct any SPAGt errors. 4. PEER review the model paragraph. 5. Give the paragraph a WWW and EBI comment	**Question focus**	**Organisation**	**Line of argument**	**Supporting information**
	The answer is consistently focused on the question. The content is very relevant and does not go off on any tangents.	The answer is well structured. All explanations are coherent throughout and examples follow relevant points made.	The line and flow of argument is very clear and concise. It is persuasive and convincing.	Supporting information demonstrates wide-ranging knowledge and understanding. It is very well selected.
	The answer is mainly focused on the question. Most content is relevant.	The answer is generally well organised. However, some parts lack coherence and seem a little jumbled at times.	The line of argument is generally clear and convincing. Overall, it is maintained through the answer.	Supporting information demonstrates good knowledge and understanding. It is generally well selected.
	The answer has weak or limited links to the question. Some content is irrelevant or unrelated.	Some points and/or statements are developed. There is some attempt to organise material consistently.	The line of argument is partly convincing. However, it is not fully maintained through the answer.	Supporting information demonstrates some knowledge and understanding. It could have better selections.
	The answer has no real links to the question. Content is confused.	The answer seems jumbled. It lacks organisation.	The line of argument is unclear, confused and/ or missing.	Supporting information is limited, irrelevant or missing.

Figure 4.7 Initial instructions for Faizah Awan's General Certificate of Secondary Education (GCSE) modelling activities

LO: To develop our responses to GCSE 12 mark questions

Practice question: Explain changes in medical knowledge during the period c.1500 – c.1700.

Model Paragraph 1

Changes in science and technology is an example of a factor that changed medical Knowledge, e.g, william harvey and andreas vesalius had new ideas in these centuries which led to new discoverys, treatments and inventions. They better understanded how our bodies worked and this improved treatments and people lived longer. These changes were very different from before. The traditional treatments and equipment was improved as well. Change happened very quickly and people become better at anatomy and giving medicine.

Figure 4.8 Faizah's first modelled answer

LO: To develop our responses to GCSE 12 mark questions.

Practice question: Explain changes in medical knowledge during the period c.1500 – c.1700.

Model Paragraph 2

One factor which led to changes in medical knowledge during the period c.1500 – c.1700 is the work of individual physicians and surgeons in improving our scientific knowledge of the human body. For instance, William Harvey studied the circulation of blood. He then taught others how blood is pumped to the brain and the rest of the body by the heart, which was a major innovation that led to other discoveries about the body and improvements in how we treat illnesses. Not only did others start to take a more scientific approach to understanding how the body functions, but physicians and surgeons started to identify causes of various diseases and considered how these diseases could be treated or even prevented. This approach to medicine broke with the more traditional methods used before the 16th century.

Figure 4.9 Faizah's second modelled answer

> **Practice homework question: Explain changes in medical knowledge during the period c.1500 – c.1700 (12 marks).**
> **You may use in your answer:**
> - the work of William Harvey
> - scientific developments made by the Royal Society

• This can be typed on Google Docs or written in your books. • You need to at least include 3 PEA paragraphs. • You must include your own evidence of wider reading as well as those suggested by the bullet points provided. • You will have around <u>15 minutes</u> to complete this in the exam	• **Step 1:** de-code the question. What is it asking you? • **Step 2:** Identify a range of factors. You will need to write about three. • **Step 3:** Organise your writing into paragraphs. • **Step 4:** 'Prove' that the factor was important – develop your explanation by using killer facts.

Figure 4.10 Faizah's final instructions setting up the practice task

Another good example of modelling and, just as importantly, scaffolding for homework retrieval practice tasks can be seen below (Figure 4.11). My son received this task from his year 4 teacher. In the first set of tasks, the pupils are given full examples of fronted adverbials, which are essentially modelled answers; they had also gone through these in class. In the second set, the activity is scaffolded as pupils are given only the main parts of the sentences; essentially, they have to choose the correct fronted adverbial from the choices in the box, which clearly – if the learner thinks about it – relate to time, frequency, place and degree. In the last set, the pupil has to add their own fronted adverbial. For set 4, the pupils simply have to practice writing their own sentences using fronted adverbials.

The above example also demonstrates Hattie and Yates's (2014) reflections on worked examples and completion examples. Essentially, the first set is a worked example, sets 2 and 3 are scaffolded completion examples and the last set is a non-scaffolded practice piece for pupils to attempt by themselves. I would still see all this as retrieval practice as the pupil is applying the schema needed to order the sentence correctly as well as associate the correct fronted adverbials (or their own made-up fronted adverbials and sentences). Getting this right with an 8-year-old takes practice, believe me!

Independent practice

The penultimate strategy suggested by Rosenshine in his *Principles of Instruction* was motivating pupils to engage in *independent practice*. Essentially, his research findings found that regular guided practice, which includes the ideas associated with modelling and scaffolding above, lays the foundations for independent practice – where pupils work alone by both

Set 1. Read the sentences. The fronted adverbials are in bold.

1. **At six o'clock in the morning,** James' alarm clock went off and he got up. *(time)*

2. **Sometimes,** dad lets us stay up to watch Match of the Day. *(frequency)*

3. **In the distance,** we could see the aeroplane coming in to land. *(place)*

4. **As quick as she could,** Alyshia ran away from the spider in the bath. *(manner)*

5. **Very energetically,** Marcus ran 100 metres and finished first. *(degree)*

Set 2. Read the sentences. The fronted adverbials are in the box. Place the correct adverbial with the rest of the sentence.

6. _____, Emma went to bed very early. *(time)*

7. _____, we get to go to the fun swim on Saturday afternoons. *(frequency)*

8. _____, dad was cooking our dinner. *(place)*

9. _____, Peter started crying. *(manner)*

10. _____, the boy scouts realised they were miles from the campsite. *(degree)*

| *Unexpectedly* | *That evening* | *Completely lost* | *Sometimes* | *In the kitchen* |

Set 3. Add your own fronted adverbials. Remember the examples from class.

11. _____, the clocks started chiming. *(time)*

12. _____, Muhammad reads to his brother. *(frequency)*

13. _____, the children were playing football. *(place)*

14. _____, Sarah started tidying her bedroom. *(manner)*

15. _____, Freddie finished the half-marathon. *(degree)*

Set 4. Write your own sentences using fronted adverbials.

16. _____, _____. *(time)*

17. _____, _____. *(frequency)*

18. _____, _____. *(place)*

19. _____, _____. *(manner)*

20. _____, _____. *(degree)*

Figure 4.11 Modelled and scaffolded fronted adverbial homework task (adapted from a Cranborne Primary School homework task)

recalling and applying what has been taught. Rosenshine stated that '[t]his independent practice is necessary because a good deal of practice (overlearning) is needed in order to become fluent and automatic in a skill' (Rosenshine, 2012, p. 18).

In relation to homework, effective teachers should have adequately guided practice to the extent that they can set independent practice tasks for homework in the knowledge that pupils have the ability to complete them. Of course, at this stage, pupils will be attempting these tasks to improve the fluency of knowledge retrieval and their skills of knowledge application to specific questions or problems. Independent practice tasks could include any of the tasks discussed above as well as subject-specific activities and problems (see, for example, Kirby, 2015).

Limitations of retrieval practice

Coe (2019) cautions teachers in their use of retrieval practice and his cautionary points can be applied to other areas of teaching and learning where teachers are enthusiastically applying ideas from cognitive psychology and science in their classrooms. Citing Dunlosky et al. (2013), Coe points out that studies often focus on simple verbal materials, which include the recall of word lists and paired associates. Here, he suggests that cognitive scientists have questioned whether retrieval practice improves performance in the face of more complex tasks. He also highlights the observation by Rohrer et al. (2019) that the impact of retrieval practice has yet to be fully demonstrated for mathematics tasks beyond fact learning. What is important here is that Coe and the researchers he cites are all in favour – to varying degrees – of retrieval practice. However, they are fully aware of the limitations of their studies and the issues of their application outside of controlled experiments in ways that many educational bloggers, writers and consultants are not. Therefore, any wholesale adaption of retrieval practice for homework does need to be approached in a contextually critical way.

Coe offers some advice that should be heeded in relation to homework. He suggests avoiding these common mistakes:

- setting retrieval-based questions that consistently focus on factual recall and do not require any higher-order thinking. Hopefully, this chapter has given some ideas on how to create retrieval practice tasks that go beyond simple recall of facts and allow for the application of skills and knowledge to questions and problems.
- setting questions that are too easy, which boost confidence but at the expense of any real challenge (this will be discussed in relation to low-stakes testing in more depth in Chapter 6)
- allocating too much time to quizzes, effectively losing the time that pupils need to cover new material. However, this last point might be where homework can act as a conduit for additional practice away from the classroom.

Lastly, I am well aware that many a cynical teacher might point out that my use of retrieval practice as homework relies on a healthy dose of trust between teacher and pupil; here, pupils will need to be trusted to complete these tasks honestly if there is to be any impact on their learning and later achievement. Whilst I accept this, I feel that any decent teacher will build up a trusting relationship with pupils through explaining the principles behind retrieval practice and acknowledging the temptation to 'cheat' whilst discouraging it. This is easier said than done in some cases, but if a pupil is inspired to learn and has high aspirations, then they will generally tend to do as they are told.

Key takeaways from Chapter 4

- It is clear that policy-makers and a fair number of educationalists – albeit not all – have been successful in championing a move towards a more 'knowledge-based curriculum'.
- The 2014 curriculum reforms have, arguably, driven in a more content-heavy curriculum, which is reflected in harder GCSE and A-level exams. Therefore, it is imperative that teachers endeavour to help pupils to retain as much of the knowledge and skills they are taught as possible.
- Our pupils' ability to retrieve information and apply it in the correct way in exams will give them increased life chances through better results.
- One way to do the above, as we have seen, is through the use of retrieval practice tasks, and there is plenty of academic and classroom-based research demonstrating the impact that these activities have on learning and achievement. Many of these can be adapted for homework, including the basic application of practice exam questions and past papers to the use of cryptic crosswords and 'thinking quilts'.
- It can be argued that homework tasks can include varied tasks and the generation effect, which research also suggests enhances the impact of retrieval practice.
- We should model and scaffold many of these tasks, so that pupils are confident enough to attempt them independently. Importantly, it is worth emphasising that retrieval practice facilitates the ideas of practice and rehearsal of previously taught knowledge highlighted in the previous chapter, in that they are the most impactful types of homework tasks.
- We should be aware of the limitations of these ideas and that we may need to adapt them to our specific contexts.

Nonetheless, retrieval practice is closely tied to some of the ideas explored in the next chapters, particularly low-stakes testing, spaced distribution and interleaving. For a fuller understanding of how these intertwine and impact on homework, please read on.

Notes

1 The Herts & Bucks Challenge Partners' Hub completed a joint research project on retrieval practice the year after the homework project (2018/2019). The schools involved met regularly to discuss ideas, evaluate the impact of any trials completed and to share best practice. The following year (2019/2020), we focused on interleaving (see Chapter 8). Some of the ideas from these projects are blogged at *Tales From The Reach*; see www.talesfromthereach.wordpress.com.
2 Answers for the anagrams: omnipotent, omniscient, omnibenevolent and omnipresent; these are all key words for the 'nature of God' topic in the AQA GCSE Religious Studies syllabus.
3 As above: Good → evil, heaven → hell, Adam → Eve, Eden → Fall, life → death, sin → salvation.

Suggested further reading

Dunlosky, J. (2013b). Strengthening the Student Toolbox: Study Strategies to Boost Learning. *The American Educator*, 37(3), 12–21.

Rosenshine, B. (2012b). Principles of Instruction: Research-Based Strategies That All Teachers Should Know. *The American Educator*, 36(1), 12–19.

Both of these articles are worth reading and are not too long. The first looks at various teaching strategies, reviews the research on them and essentially ranks them in order of effectiveness. The second looks at the way we deliver certain strategies and gives 10 (with an additional box in the text listing 17) effective strategies on teaching and learning. Retrieval practice is central to both articles.

Jones, K. (2019). *Retrieval Practice: Research and Resources for Every Classroom*. Woodbridge, VA: John Catt Publications.

Kate Jones gives a good overview of the research on retrieval practice and champions its use in the classroom. The book contains a number of useful strategies for use in the classroom (and even for homework). Essentially, a good introductory primer on the subject.

5 Preparation, flipped learning and independent learning

Chapter overview

This chapter focuses on types of *preparation task* and gives some examples of their use. It also considers *flipped learning* as preparation and why we should take a cautious approach despite much fanfare from its advocates. The chapter moves on to offer advice on preparing pupils for assessments and exams through homework, which includes a discussion on *independent learning* as revision and the role of *metacognition* and *meta-learning* in preparation tasks.

I hate being unprepared. Not knowing what is going on or what I need to do is both disorientating and disconcerting in everyday life let alone in the classroom. In fact, our Teacher Standards suggest that we need to be fully prepared, including having planned and resourced our lessons as well as adapting these plans and resources to the needs of the pupils we teach. It is incumbent for us to impart the importance of preparation onto our pupils. Homework, of course, is one way of doing this. We saw in Chapter 2 how many researchers, including Cooper (2007) and Hallam and Rogers (2018), identify preparation tasks as one of the more impactful ways of setting homework and we also found out that some studies, such as Bempechat (2004), suggest that homework can help pupils develop good study skills and habits; being prepared is a key example of an effective habit. Therefore, preparation homework tasks have two key uses: one is to get pupils ready for future lessons and to save precious time in class by having pupils go over key areas of study beforehand; the other is the practice of study skills associated with preparation, such as research methods, revision strategies and self-regulation in completing work adequately enough *to be prepared*.

Types of preparation tasks

It goes without saying that some of the strategies used in preparation will overlap with the retrieval practice ideas discussed in the previous chapter. Nonetheless, key preparation tasks could include the following:

- reading ahead, including set texts or relevant textbook chapters
- learning key vocabulary needed in an upcoming lesson
- taking notes on materials that will be used in class activities
- making a list of questions to have answered in class by the teacher
- making a list of questions to have answered in class by other pupils
- making a list of questions that pupils will have to answer in class through assigned activities
- researching and summarising a key event, concept or issue that will be further studied in class, perhaps in far more depth by the teacher
- researching and summarising a key event, concept or issue that will be discussed and debated in class
- producing handouts, guides or presentation slides on a topic that will be discussed in class
- finding items that might be needed in practical subjects; this could include shapes for geometry in primary classes or appropriate objects for still-life drawings in art lessons
- of course, pupils could apply any of the ideas used in the previous chapter to prepare for upcoming tests or exams.

All of these tasks need to be considered in the context of the pupils you teach. It is all too easy to set simplistic preparation tasks that do not get pupils to challenge themselves. Moreover, it is important to pitch tasks at the right level; if centred on too much new information or subject knowledge, tasks that require pupils to read ahead might cognitively overload them. Also, where new material is used, such as learning new vocabulary in a foreign language, subject content should not be too disconnected from the unit of learning or sequence of lessons; pupils should be able to use these words to build on their previous learning.

Supporting pupils to prepare for upcoming lessons through homework

One of the issues with preparation tasks is a lack of structure. Whereas learning 10 words for a spelling test next lesson is quite straightforward, telling pupils to create a handout for their peers is more ambiguous. It is essential, then, that tasks be set up with easy-to-understand instructions as well as supporting materials if needed. However, any materials should also be relatively straightforward to use and should prevent cognitive load (see Chapter 7).

- Ensure that your homework instructions are clear. Explain why the pupils need to do this homework. This will involve time in class and should not be rushed at the end as pupils start putting things away, scrape their chair legs on the floor as they stand up and prepare to whizz out the door.

- Give pupils plenty of time to prepare. Unless the preparation tasks are very short, such as learning five key terms overnight, you need to factor in research time or how long it will take to organise themselves.
- Give pupils guidance on how to use any preparation materials. For instance, 'Please read pages 43–45 of the textbook for next lesson' as opposed to 'Please read ahead'.
- Consider pupils' learning needs. Although differentiation is discussed in Chapter 9, you may need to consider some pupils' ability to complete all of the preparation tasks. For example, do they need differentiated texts or simplified instructions?
- Provide pupils with a checklist if there are a number of tasks. For example, if pupils need to produce a presentation for their peers in the next lesson, you may need to include a checklist of key parts of the presentation, such as an introduction and conclusion or the formalities expected in the speech.
- Provide pupils with a glossary of technical words and terms. This might be useful if pupils need to prepare for upcoming written assignments or vocabulary tests.

Given the above, it is important to model and scaffold preparation tasks if the strategies applied are new to pupils. This is in a similar vein to the discussion on modelling and scaffolding in the previous chapter, as pupils will need the subject-specific skills to prepare effectively. For instance, if pupils are to read ahead and make notes, are these merely copied or summarised in the pupils' own words after reading? (The latter is more effective.) If pupils are to learn a new set of times tables or key words, do they prepare by rote learning or do they make flash cards or apply techniques discussed in the previous chapter, perhaps covering up definitions and recalling by elaboration or mixing up (interleaving) the times table in a different order? This would be a desirable difficulty.

Flipped learning as preparation: take a cautious approach

Quite a few of my colleagues recommend *flipped learning* as an approach to homework. Although some swear by it, I am a little uneasy with the concept as a whole. This is because the learning that normally takes place in the classroom takes place in the home and I am unsure whether pupils can really benefit from direct instruction without the teacher present. However, proponents see flipped learning as a way of blending traditional teaching methods with modern technology; therefore, some refer to it as a form of *blended learning*. Essentially, a lot of the initial instruction and explanation needed in a lesson or sequence of lessons can take place away from the classroom through videos, voice recordings or written explanations; this means that teachers have more time in class to support pupils in various activities that can support their learning, which could include practice tasks, or discuss their learning individually or in groups. Moreover, this approach frees up time for class discussion and debate as well as pair and group work. It could also pave the way for more creative activities in the classroom, including role plays and artwork, for example.

Advocates of flipped learning (and its variants, such as *peer learning* or *inverted class-rooms*), including Mazur (1997), Lage, Platt and Treglia (2000) and Mazur, Brown and Jacobsen (2015), emphasise the importance of freeing up learning for a range of in-class activities and support that are limited in the 'traditional classroom'. Here, November and Mull (2012, p. 1) suggest that flipped learning has these core components:

- Pupils prepare for lessons in class by watching videos, listening to recordings/podcasts, reading texts or considering questions based on previous learning.
- Pupils then consider questions or identify issues to address in the class with the teacher or peers.
- Pupils then use an online discussion tool, such as a virtual learning environment like Google Classroom, to post questions for the teacher to review prior to the actual class-based lesson.
- The teacher uses the above to help plan the lesson.
- In the actual class-based lesson, the teacher can use the Socratic method of teaching; here, questions and problems are posed and pupils discuss these before working either in collaboration or on activities that help them answer the questions and solve the problems posed.
- The teacher can circulate the classroom and help pupils individually or in small groups.

However, there are considerable questions about this approach. First, Lo and Hew point out that '[t]he major problems of using flipped classroom approach include teachers' considerable workload of creating flipped learning materials, and students' disengagement in the out-of-class learning' (2017, p. 2). Indeed, teachers will need to not only prepare the content for flipped learning but also video or record themselves if offering pupils recorded instructions, which arguably would require an additional period of teaching. Moreover, Li (2018) suggests that as the best way to deliver flipped learning content is technology-centred, many teachers do not have the computer or information technology knowledge or skills to put together impactful flipped learning resources. Yes, they acknowledge that it is possible to give out worksheets and readings to prepare pupils for future lessons, but this is not really conducive to the core idea of instructing pupils in subject knowledge away from the classroom.

Li, building on the research of Wang (2009) and Dai (2016), goes on to suggest that whilst technology, including smartphones, is an ideal way to facilitate collaboration away from the classroom, it is not always conducive to facilitating pupils' attention to the tasks at hand. Not only will they be tempted to get side-tracked by social media, pupils could end up plagiarising information from the internet or simply become lazy and less 'business-like' in their approach to the flipped learning tasks. Essentially, 'Without supervision, students use their smartphones more for fun than for study's sake' (Li, 2018, p. 9). It was also evident that many studies, reviewed by Li, demonstrated that videos often were too long or too in-depth for pupils to remain focused; some pupils even stated that they preferred the 'traditional' approach to teaching in class.

It is worth mentioning that some – but not all – of the early proponents of flipped learning saw it as a way to focus on pupils' learning styles (see Lage, Platt and Treglia, 2000, for instance), which is a largely discredited approach to teaching and learning, or as a way of facilitating pupil-centred learning, which has also been questioned in various studies as being less impactful than supposedly more traditional approaches to teaching and learning; for discussions on this, see Christodoulou (2013) and Didau (2016).

That said, there is no reason why teachers cannot adapt some of the ideas of flipped learning to support pupils' preparation homework tasks. It may be that instructional videos or voice recordings are limited and used to aid pupils in the pronunciation of vocabulary that needs learning or that videos are used to reinforce key concepts. Importantly, these videos do not need to be excessive and any impactful teacher will check how well pupils understood these in following lessons. It may be that flipped learning, particularly if viewed as a form of preparation, is useful in some subjects more than others. My colleague Ralph Addy, whose computer studies General Certificate of Secondary Education (GCSE) results are some of the best in the school, applies flipped learning effectively in his lessons. Ralph gets pupils to come to class prepared with a strategy to implement in the lesson that they have picked up from his remote learning resources. This means pupils can use their valuable lesson time coding or sequencing programmes whilst Ralph checks for mistakes and misconceptions, which – if not picked up early – can frustrate pupils as their programming will not work. (See Table 5.1 for the pros and cons of flipped learning.)

Table 5.1 The pros and cons of flipped learning

Pros of flipped learning	Cons of flipped learning

• Gives pupils flexibility in terms of when to study
• Pupils can work at their own pace.
• Teachers can offer choice in how pupils complete work, especially if the teacher sets up different tasks.
• Resources and materials are available for pupils who missed lessons.
• Frees up lesson time for discussion and debate
• Frees up time for activities that arguably promote 'higher-order thinking skills'
• Allows lessons to be given over to collaborative or group activities
• Could allow for more creative activities in class time as well as 'pupil-centred learning'
• Allows teachers to spend more time with pupils one-to-one or in small groups
• Could free up time in lessons for more practice-based activities, including guided practice
• Allows more time for assessment and feedback in class
• Allows pupils to develop independent study skills
	• Pupils might not understand the content taught via videos or slides.
	• Pupils cannot ask questions at the time of learning, which is made more pertinent as flipped learning is focused on instruction, not practice.
	• Teachers cannot tell whether pupils are engaged with their instructional materials at the time.
	• Time management is an issue; whereas practice homework tasks can be quick, instructional activities might be longer.
	• Longer homework tasks are impacted by the curvilinear effect (see Chapter 2).
	• Pupils' attention spans might be affected by
	  o the home environment
	  o other aspects of the technologies they are using, such as social media.
	• Pupils might not have the right equipment to engage with flipped learning.
	• Technology is an obstacle to flipped learning; do pupils have the devices and internet connections needed?
	• Teachers will have to spend considerable time preparing these materials.

Independent learning: preparation for assessments and exams (a.k.a. revision)

Moving beyond standalone preparation tasks that can be set with a specific goal in mind, such as 'read Chapter 5 of *Animal Farm* for next week', or even flipped learning for specific areas of study, we need to consider preparation for assessments and exams. In this sense, preparation can be seen as revision as pupils might be set a series of homework tasks in the run-up to significant summative assessments or public exams, such as GCSEs or A levels. A key element of this longer-term preparation will hinge on pupils being able to work independently. Here, *independent learning* is when an individual pupil has the ability and motivation to think about what they need to learn outside of lessons and then put those thoughts into action. However, pupils will need to know what to focus on and use the correct resources without constant guidance from their teachers. Pupils will also need to use learning strategies that are proven to improve their subject knowledge and skills. There is arguably an overlap here with some of the retrieval practice strategies explained in the previous chapter. I would argue that pupils should see independent learning, especially in the run-up to exams, as *independent practice*. Whether practising the retrieval of knowledge or the application of skills, pupils can use independent practice to help them prepare for assessments and exams by honing their academic abilities.

Although their understanding of independent learning encompasses more than my emphasis on independent practice, researchers have found that independent learning benefits pupils in a number of ways. For example, Meyer et al. (2008, pp. 1-2) pinpoint six key benefits in their literature review of research into independent learning. The benefits for pupils include the following:

- improved overall academic performance
- increased motivation and confidence
- greater pupil awareness of their limitations and whether they can manage them
- enabling teachers to provide differentiated tasks for them, especially as these can be completed over longer time frames than lessons
- giving pupils a sense of social inclusion by countering a sense of alienation.

In light of the above, it would be an understatement to say that sound independent learning skills are transferable to homework, but I am going to make that point anyway. Basically, if you want your pupils to prepare for assessments and exams effectively, you must help them master the skills of autonomous study prior to the revision period in the run-up to exams. Here, research on metacognition and metalearning is useful and demonstrates how independent study skills can be more impactful in terms of learning and achievement if pupils *know why it helps them learn* (see Practitioner Research Box 5.1, for instance).

Metacognition and metalearning

According to Seng, Tey and Fam (1993), *metacognition* is thinking about thinking. Here, a pupil would need to plan, monitor and review their own thinking and approach to learning. *Metalearning*, on the other hand, is thinking about learning. In the process of metalearning, pupils are deliberately aware that they are in control of their own learning, especially in

Practitioner Research Box 5.1
Laura Curtis - What are the principal characteristics of challenging
and meaningful homework tasks when trying to engage and extend the
understanding of learners at Key Stage 5?

The aim of Laura's Herts & Bucks Challenge Partners' Hub/CamStar research was to discover what effective and impactful homework looks like at Key Stage 5. To achieve this, she identified a range of homework strategies that could be trialed across a number of A-level subjects. Both the pupils and staff involved had to complete survey questions before and after the trials to allow the value of the homework set to be assessed; this was based on their experiences.

Laura writes that the pupil survey was extremely insightful in terms of attitudes towards homework and how useful pupils find it. Interestingly, both the staff survey and the pupil survey found that the main purpose of homework is to consolidate learning or to practice a skill in preparation for exams. When pupils were asked to give reasons for why they do not complete homework, many stated that they end up prioritising their homework because of time constraints and therefore homework that they do not see as valuable ends up being ignored. As a result, independent and exam-based homework tasks were seen as 'most valuable' and this was corroborated by the opinions of the staff involved in the trial. When structured clearly and prepared effectively, lesson preparation and flipped learning are also valuable strategies, but the rationale behind such tasks must be made clear. In order to remove any barriers affecting the completion of homework, shorter tasks were seen as preferable with the purpose of tasks clearly articulated to the pupils so that they can see the benefit of what they are doing. Laura suggests that if such an approach can be developed consistently across A-level teaching, it will ensure that pupils are engaged with their homework, which will serve to extend their understanding and prepare learners effectively for their A-level exams.

Of course, this research was contextual to the school in question.

Laura is a history teacher and Lead Teacher for Teaching and Learning at Chesham Grammar School, Chesham, Buckinghamshire.

terms of organising strategies and approaches towards studying as well as pre-emptively identifying likely mistakes and evaluating their performance. Of the two terms, metacognition is commonly used in relation to teaching and learning. However, although I will start with metacognition and its importance to preparation homework tasks, I think the less common term metalearning is still worth discussing afterwards.

A whole host of studies have shown how metacognition and self-regulation impact on school performance. For example, one study demonstrated that '[d]ifferent areas of self-regulation could explain 34% of variance of school performance in the primary school, about 21% in the secondary school and nearly 14% in university education' (Vukman & Licardo, 2010, p. 267). Another study found that there 'is strong evidence indicating that when metacognition is effectively taught in schools then there is a very positive effect on pupil outcomes' (Perry, Lundie & Golder, 2019, p. 483). It is clear, then, that we should consider the processes that develop metacognitive skills in our pupils. Beyer (1987, cited in Seng, Tey & Fam, 1993) suggests that the key processes involved in metacognition are planning (including goal setting, sequencing operations and identifying obstacles), monitoring (including keeping an awareness of the goals set and operational sequences planned as well as obstacles) and assessing (including assessing whether the goal has been achieved, judging the accuracy of this achievement and evaluating the efficiency of the tasks used).

Importantly, in 2018, the Education Endowment Foundation (EEF) developed similar guidance for teachers in schools. Their advice is helpful as it underpins the importance of highlighting metacognition as an explicit learning strategy to be used in our primary and secondary schools. Their guidance can be broken down into three broad areas (EEF, 2018, p. 6):

1. That we should acquire a professional understanding of the skills needed to develop our pupils' metacognition, including the following:
   - helping pupils become self-regulated learners who can assess their own strengths and weaknesses
   - developing pupils' metacognitive understanding of how they learn, which includes knowledge of effective learning strategies
   - supporting pupils to plan, monitor and evaluate their learning (in a vein similar to Byer above).
2. That we should actually teach metacognitive strategies to pupils; this involves the following:
   - explicitly teaching pupils how metacognitive strategies can improve their learning and achievement
   - ensuring that these strategies are not overly generic and relate to the nuanced context of their learning; here, metacognition in maths might be different from drama, for example
   - that the above are taught in a series of steps, which include using prior knowledge, independent practice and finally reflection; again, this needs to be considered within the context of the subject and age group.
3. That we should model our own thinking to develop pupils' metacognition, such as the following:
   - revealing our own thought processes
   - verbalising the above points where possible (this is essentially thinking aloud)
   - guiding pupils through scaffolded tasks, such as worked examples.

Although the EEF guidance mostly referred to learning *per se*, I feel that these metacognitive skills, or processes, are a prerequisite to successful preparation homework, especially in the case of revision. Gone are the days when we would just expect our pupils to get on with revision, which would probably involve copious amounts of reading and re-reading. In fact, some of the strategies discussed in the previous chapter would need to be regularly flagged up by teachers as possible revision techniques to counter the academic naivety of simply re-reading the same text over and over again. As suggested already, here we see some clear overlap between the strategies suggested (in the previous chapter) by Dunlosky (2013), who is referenced in the EEF guidance, and pupils' own understanding of which strategies have the most impact on learning.

At The Reach Free School, we not only encourage homework tasks based on retrieval practice (or even practice as preparation) but also advocate its use for revision purposes in the run-up to significant class assessments, mock exams or the summer GCSE and A-level exams (see Figure 5.1, for example). Here, pupils are taught these 'revision skills', which can be used either independently or as part of directed revision tasks. Again, these skills include a number of ideas advocated by Dunlosky et al. (2013) as 'very effective' but also build upon some of the less effective ones by making them into practice of preparation activities.

Moreover, in relation to the research on homework discussed in Chapter 2, self-regulation and the ability to manage workload are essential for preparation tasks that may be set over longer periods than tasks set from lesson to lesson. Revision is literally going over everything the pupils have studied throughout their course of study, so it is self-evident that if your pupils can organise themselves and get studying without the help of a teacher, this process will be much easier and simpler for them. This is essential as you cannot possibly revise everything with your pupils; they will have to do most of it alone.

So, how is metacognition different from metalearning and what has this got to do with preparation tasks? Basically, they are similar, but metalearning is '[t]he process by which learners become aware of and increasingly in control of habits of perception, inquiry, learning, and growth that they have internalized' (Maudsley, 1979, cited in Mezirow, 1981). In this sense, the more that pupils become familiar with the processes and strategies of metacognition, the more they will become aware of how these impact on their learning over time. They will also become apt at applying them in the context of their subjects, perhaps using specific strategies in one subject and different strategies in another (Jackson, 2004).

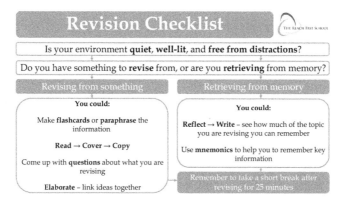

Figure 5.1 A revision checklist (designed by Martyn Essery)

Breaking this down, Seng, Tey and Fam (1993, p. 4) suggest that metalearning enables pupils to:

- estimate and monitor their competence in finishing a task
- plan and organise strategies to solve a problem
- select and apply appropriate strategies
- identify and correct mistakes
- evaluate their overall performance on completing a task
- plan for independent study and revision.

The last point is significant as it takes us back to the first term cited in this section, albeit in relation to teaching pupils how to learn independently as opposed to traditional study or revision where pupils simply go over or re-read material. If we are to get pupils to prepare for upcoming lessons via homework, then it makes sense for us to employ the processes and strategies of metacognition, even in small tasks between lessons, before starting to piece together how these ideas can be applied in different ways in different contexts or subject areas. In this sense, we are getting them to be independent in both their learning and, of course, practice. However, one issue is still self-regulation; this might fall into place for some pupils, but for others they may still need additional support, especially if preparation tasks are set over a series of lessons as pupils approach assessments and exams.

Supporting pupils with preparation for assessments and exams: revision aids

One way to help pupils plan their independent study or revision in the run-up to exams is to use unit booklets with recommended reading lists and audit tools for analysing their strengths and weaknesses, which is a metacognitive skill. Many schools now insist that teachers produce *personal learning checklists* for their pupils. Table 5.2 gives an example of one of these, which is based on a scheme of work introducing pupils to key sociological perspectives; it also links to a larger booklet with retrieval practice tasks in it as well as multiple-choice quizzes. These tables allow the pupils to check what they have learnt and where their weaknesses are in terms of subject knowledge. I encourage them to 'triage' or rank what they know most about and what they know least when using Table 5.3. You can also use this to get them planning how much revision time they will need for these areas. The booklet incorporating these tables includes a glossary without definitions (see Table 5.4), which the pupils will need to recall themselves (this last example is for a crime-and-punishment unit in religious education, not sociology). The point of this exam preparation/revision task is to get pupils finding information themselves as they go through the unit. You can give them websites in addition to further reading to help them with this. Importantly, if the pupils feel they are weak in a particular area of the unit (or wider syllabus) or if they feel they have no clue what a key word is, then they are aware that they should basically knuckle down to some hard study and find out.

Table 5.2 A personal learning checklist used in sociology (adapted from Jones, 2017)

Unit 1: Introduction to sociology

Unit 1	Brief content	Completed handbook?	Done quiz?	R	A	G	Brief comments
What is sociology? Social norms	Outline of the course, meaning of sociology, key issues etc. Explanation of social norms, values, rules and status as well as social identity etc.						
Socialisation Functionalism	Explanation of socialisation, including primary and secondary. Durkheim, organic analogy, Talcott Parsons, social control, consensus.						
Marxism	Karl Marx, infrastructure, superstructure, class conflict, exploitation, false consciousness.						
Feminism	Liberal feminism, Marxist feminism, radical feminism, black feminism.						
Social action theory/ interactionist theory	Max Weber, Verstehen, meanings, micro theory, labelling.						
New right Postmodernism	Charles Murray, underclass, individualism, neo-liberalism. Premodernity, modernity, postmodernity, fragmentation, identity, hybridity.						
Social perspectives review	Micro, macro, structural, social action, conflict, consensus.						

Table 5.3 A unit reflection log used in sociology (adapted from Jones, 2017)

Topic	Exam-confident?	Areas of strength and/or improvement
The Functionalist view of the role of education in society	Yes or No	
The Marxist view of the role of education in society	Yes or No	
The Feminist view of the role of education in society	Yes or No	
The New Right View of the role of education	Yes or No	
The Postmodernist view of education	Yes or No	
Exam practice	Yes or No	

Table 5.4 A do-it-yourself glossary used in religious education

Key word	Write in your definition
Capital punishment	
Community service order	
Conscience	
Corporal punishment	
Crime	
Deterrence	
Duty	
Evil	
Forgiveness	

As the main exams approach, pupils need to use these booklets, re-evaluate their strengths and weaknesses as part of their exam preparation and revision planning, and complete any gaps.

Key takeaways from Chapter 5

- Building on the idea that practice and preparation tasks are the most impactful types of homework, we can see that preparation, like practice, can take many forms.
- There are plenty of tasks we can set our pupils to prepare for a lesson, including very simplistic instructions to learn some spellings to more complicated instructions to produce a presentation for their peers.
- Preparation tasks need clear explicit instructions: perhaps a concise checklist and a clear purpose in relation to the wider unit of learning or sequence of lessons.
- We have also evaluated the idea of flipped learning, which has a place in education but must be approached with caution. There are a number of technical obstacles in this approach and some clear concerns about pupils' attention and potential boredom if 'flipped classrooms' are set up poorly. There is also the issue of time and resources, which could impact on pupils – remember the curvilinear issue of time in Chapter 2 – as well as issues for teacher workload. A lot of initial studies on flipped learning came from higher education; with this in mind, note that the learning context, particularly in terms of age, is important here.

- Preparation tasks can be set between lessons as well as over time. However, if pupils are given longer to prepare, then the lack of structure and issues of self-regulation can become concerns.
- It is worth considering approaches to learning that teach metacognitive skills and strategies that make pupils aware of not only 'thinking about thinking' (metacognition) but how they learn more generally (metalearning). Perhaps a good place to start is with the Education Endowment Foundation (EEF, 2018) guidance on metacognition – many of the ideas advocated can be used to model learning in the classroom for the benefit learning at home.
- Metacognition and metalearning can really impact on pupils' learning away from the classroom, especially as they progress through school when the importance of independent study skills and revision techniques become all the more pertinent.

Suggested further reading

The EEF *Metacognition and Self-Regulated Guidance Report* (2018). Retrieved from: https://educationen-dowmentfoundation.org.uk/public/files/Publications/Metacognition/EEF_Metacognition_and_self-regulated_learning.pdf [8 July 2020].
As explained above, this research-informed guidance is relevant to the teaching of all pupils, within any subject area and at all stages of learning. Most of the practical examples and small case studies included are from Key Stages 1 to 4. It introduces a simplified framework for self-regulated learning and metacognition, which is a useful starting point.
12 Resources for Flipped Learning (ASCD InService). Retrieved from: https://inservice.ascd.org/12-resources-on-flipped-learning/ [6 July 2020].
The ASCD have a list of resources, mostly by Jonathan Bergmann and Aaron Sams but also including Cathy Vatterott, on flipped learning. Some are free and others are recommended books. These resources explain the processes and strategies behind flipped learning and suggest that teachers should move away from direct instruction as their primary teaching method towards a more pupil-centred approach. However, although this list is useful, I would still approach it with a critical mind as other research suggests otherwise.

6 Checking homework, assessment and feedback

Chapter overview

This chapter will consider why *checking learning* is an essential follow-up to homework and looks at different ways of checking that it has been completed, including *questioning* pupils and *low-stakes testing*. The chapter then examines how to best assess homework and emphasises the importance of feedback, particularly *whole-class feedback*.

Mrs. Dawson set maths homework every week. It was not much. Normally, if my memory serves me correctly, she would set about 20 questions from the topic we were studying. I never did these questions. Sometimes, I would see whether my friend Ben had completed them and then frantically try to copy his answers down in form time. Annoyingly, we would have to self-assess our answers in class as Mrs. Dawson circulated the classroom seeing what we had done. Therefore, in most lessons, I would go into class, get out a piece of paper, cup my hand over it and pretend to tick my questions whilst I was really writing down the answers as they were read out. I would not get them all right, of course, and I made sure some were wrong. Invariably, we would get to question 16 or 17 and I would entertain the idea that I had got away with doing nothing and would not have the company of my maths teacher at break time. And then, as always, she would appear at my shoulder, give a moan of disappointment, swipe away the paper and I would lose my lunch break.

Checking homework: essentially checking learning

In relation to homework, Rosenshine (2012) discusses how daily or weekly *reviews*, which were briefly mentioned in Chapter 4, can be used to check homework, particularly checking for mistakes or misconceptions in the pupils' use of terms, concepts or skills. Importantly, if pupils are to use either preparation activities or retrieval practice strategies to complete homework tasks, these will need to be reviewed either through checking or low-stakes testing. Straightforward strategies like peer assessment can be used in conjunction with questioning and discussion on the parts of the homework that pupils find difficult or perhaps where they made similar mistakes. Subsequently, Rosenshine suggests that teachers could use *daily review* activities to do the following:

- Correct any mistakes and misunderstandings in pupils' homework
- Review the concepts and skills practised for homework
- Ask pupils about any difficulties they had in completing the homework or errors made
- Review the content where errors occurred
- Lastly, '[r]eview material that needs overlearning (i.e., newly acquired skills should be practiced well beyond the point of initial mastery, leading to automaticity)'.

(ibid., p. 2)

Checking can happen in a number of ways. Here are some key practices to check that pupils have completed their homework.

Circulation. Quite simply, you should get out of the chair and walk around the room and literally look at the pupils' homework. Granted, this will not involve all pupils if you want to actually check their work in-depth, but getting sight of the tasks set is a quick way of at least seeing who has done what – remember Mrs. Dawson!

Targeted Q&A. This will be discussed below but essentially involves asking questions that elicit whether pupils have completed their homework tasks.

Low-stakes testing. These can be used to ensure that preparation and practice tasks have impacted on pupils' learning as well as help teachers identify gaps in knowledge in addition to pupils' overall weaknesses in recalling what was covered in their homework.

Self- or peer-assessment. Get pupils to self- or peer-assess homework tasks to do exactly as Rosenshine suggests above. It also saves you the hassle of marking them. Once these are assessed, marks can be written down on mini-whiteboards and held up, giving you a measure of how well the pupils did overall. Essentially, peer-assessment means that pupils will be paired and required to swap their homework tasks; assessing can be via teacher instruction or a simplified mark scheme. Similarly, pupils can mark their own homework whilst listening to the teacher or following the mark scheme if self-assessment is used.

Mini-whiteboards. Get pupils to select parts of their homework to write and hold up; you could also select random questions set for homework and ask pupils to quickly write their answers and hold them up. This works well for preparation homework as you can ask probing questions and check pupils responses, but you do run the risk of pupils writing the correct or interesting answers regardless of homework compilation. These can also be used with hinge questions, which are discussed below.

RAG cards. Many pupils have RAG cards in their planners or they can make them. These are simple red, amber and green cards that pupils can hold up or leave on the table to indicate whether they are understanding the homework tasks set. Here, green is 'understood' and red indicates they are struggling (or have not completed their homework). Although pupils might lie here or be afraid to indicate the truth, many will show red if needs be, which means you can either help them or get a sense of who has not completed their homework.

Games. Games can be a good way of checking the learning of key words or even concepts. Moreover, there are many good retrieval practice games out there; for a good exposition of these, see Jones (2019).

Questioning pupils about their homework

Researchers have estimated that teachers ask up to 400 questions each day (Leven & Long, 1981); this means that many of us ask around 70,000 a year and possibly 3 million throughout our careers. Therefore, it can be argued that questioning is one of the most important strategies a teacher has to help pupils learn. Nonetheless, despite lots of advice and debate about questioning, it is clear that some questioning strategies are more impactful than others. This suggests that our appraisal of pupils' homework may benefit from some forms of questioning more than others.

The biggest debate seems to centre on whether we should ask closed and concise questions, which are often used to ascertain pupils' knowledge of facts and figures, or open questions, which allow more elaborate and wide-ranging answers. However, there seems to be a time and a place for both of these types (Lee & Kinzie, 2012). To suggest that one type is better than another is a false dichotomy (unless used in a particular context) (see Table 6.1).

Table 6.1 Uses of open and closed questions

Closed questions	Open questions
• Closed questions can check how well the pupils have retained the subject knowledge covered by preparation tasks or applied this knowledge through practice homework tasks.	• Samson et al. (1987) found that higher-cognitive questioning strategies have a positive effect on learning. This could be particularly useful if abstract concepts have been covered in the homework tasks.
• Closed questions are quick and can be used as part of daily reviews without encroaching too much on precious lesson time.	• Open or divergent questions encourage greater expansion in answers and promote better classroom dialogue (Elder & Paul,
• These questions can allow the teacher to get a sense of formative progress (Quigley, 2012), including the extent that homework has impacted on that progress.	2002; Tofade et al., 2013). This could be useful in applying preparation activities effectively in class, especially in subjects like English. Strategies like 'think-pair-share' are
• Lower-attaining pupils benefit from closed questions, allowing them greater accuracy of response, which in turn breeds encouragement (Woolfolk et al., 2008). A competent teacher will target specific questions at certain pupils according to ability. This will allow the teacher to see whether a pupil's answers measure up to their expectations of that pupil.	useful here in developing pupils' articulation and argumentation.
	• Open questioning promotes 'higher-order thinking skills' and can be mapped against Bloom's taxonomy (Anderson et al., 2001; Doherty, 2017). As above, this could be useful in assessing how pupils have understood the homework tasks they were
• Lemov (2015) observes that 'call and response' closed questioning facilitates engaging academic review in classrooms.	set, especially if abstract or evaluative in nature.

Thinking time and hands down

One clear area of consensus is on thinking time, and many In-Service Education and Training (INSET) sessions currently involve trainers referencing 'pose, pause, pone, bounce', 'cold calling' and 'think-pair-share' amongst other strategies. (I won't outline these here, but an internet search will give you all the explanation you need if you are unfamiliar with them.) There is a good reason for this. For example, Brooks and Brooks (2001; cited in Doherty, 2017) found that a rapid-fire questioning approach fails to provide teachers with accurate information about pupil understanding and that the typical time between asking a question and a pupil's response is about one second. Here, some researchers recommend *think times* or *wait times* of at least three to five seconds for closed questions and up to 15 seconds for open-ended questions (Rowe, 1986; Stahl, 1990; Cohen et al., 2004). Lastly, studies suggest encouraging pupils to critically think through a situation, scenario or problem before giving them the solution (Cotton, 2001; Elder & Paul, 2002). Therefore, if we are checking how much our pupils have taken in at home and if we consider the small time lag between taking in information or practising a particular skill, we should give them adequate time to retrieve and organise their thoughts.

Almost all research advocates *hands-down* as opposed to hands-up questioning. For instance, the former type of questioning can do the following: allow the teacher to pause so that pupils have some thinking time; be targeted according to ability and give a sense of progress; be used to prevent passive learning by uninterested, apathetic or lazy pupils; bypass pupils' fears of being seen as a 'know-it-all', 'boffin' or 'geek' (Galton, 2002; Jackson, 2014); and encourage equitable contributions and promote equality (Harris and Williams, 2012); lastly, some hands-down questioning can be mixed with hands-up so long as pupils know that they may still be chosen (Connor, 2001).

Researchers and writers on this also tend to argue that teachers should do the following: plan ahead – think about potential questions to ask the pupils in order to thoroughly check that the homework was understood or to ascertain whether tasks are complete (Lemov, 2015); keep the language you use to ask the question straightforward, concise and easy to comprehend (even for complex open-ended questions); never embarrass pupils or be sarcastic, especially as they would have completed their homework without a teacher present; stay focused – if you or a pupil goes off on a rambling or wide-ranging tangent, you may lose the interest of the rest of the pupils who could become passive and apathetic – also, you are basically checking their homework, so this should not use up too much lesson time.

Low-stakes testing

Research has shown that *low-stakes testing* can have a significant impact on knowledge retention (Bain, 2014; Roediger, 2013). For teachers, frequent low-stakes tests can help us understand our pupils' and classes' areas of strength and development, which inevitably helps us plan a more impactful intervention; this would include whether they have been making sense of what we set for homework. In fact, research carried out by Roediger et al. (2011) suggests that there are at least 10 benefits of using low-stakes testing:

- 'the testing effect' – testing is a form of retrieval practice that aids better retention
- identifying gaps in pupils' learning/knowledge
- pupils learning more in following lessons or sequence of lessons
- improving pupils' organisation of knowledge
- improving pupils' metacognitive monitoring
- improving the transfer of knowledge to new contexts, especially if tests rephrase questions or apply source material to different contexts
- opportunities for retrieval practice/recall of knowledge (even if not specifically tested)
- preventing interference when learning new material that was not tested
- providing feedback to teachers, especially in relation to pupils' progress
- encouraging pupils to learn (as they want to improve their scores).

The Reach Free School (TRFS) included 'low-stakes testing' in our School Development Plan for 2019/2020. Research demonstrates that low-stakes testing should be part of our everyday classroom practice and, as we are a school that focuses on evidence-informed best practice, we feel that it should be championed across the school and in all subject areas and as a way of checking homework too. Moreover, there is nothing to stop teachers from setting low-stakes tests for homework, especially if you feel that you can trust your pupils to complete it without 'cheating'.

There are a number of key principles to consider when planning low-stakes tests. These principles are outlined below.

- The idea of the test being 'low-stakes' is essential; it should not be a pass-or-fail assessment and should avoid creating unnecessary anxiety and stress. You are simply seeing whether your pupils understood the homework tasks or knowledge learnt away from the classroom.
- Low-stakes testing is a great way of getting pupils to retrieve information and track whether pupils remember key aspects of the subject taught. Having a codified (written-down) list of knowledge, such as medium-term plans/schemes of learning, is your starting point. This means you can plan low-stakes tests around your plans and schemes, which include what you set for homework.
- Academic research shows that the 'testing effect' helps with knowledge retention, which relates back to the work of Dunlosky et al. (2013) discussed in Chapter 4; however, pupils do need to have spaced tests over time to combat the so-called 'forgetting curb' (see the next chapter). Here, testing involves active thinking and pupils are required to recall information (as opposed to re-learn it). It is therefore argued that this helps them commit subject knowledge to their long-term memory.
- Setting low-stakes tests can give useful insight into pupil/class strengths and areas for development. Although these tests are not assessments, you could record the scores separately to inform you of gaps in learning; if you are testing pupils on what they learnt at home, this would also indicate whether the homework task set has been understood.

Types of low-stakes testing for checking homework can include the following:

- Multiple-choice quizzes on the topics covered in the homework; there are apps that allow you to set these for homework too (see below).
- Quick quiz. Pupils answer questions in their books on an area of homework; these are ideal for checking preparation homework and can be used as practice homework if you trust your pupils not to look up answers; these quizzes are exceedingly easy to put together (see Figure 6.1).
- Key word definitions. Pupils match up the key vocabulary learnt for homework with the correct definitions; this is ideal for checking preparation tasks; for example, you could use a worksheet where pupils draw lines or even create a card sort.
- Vocabulary tests/spelling tests checking preparation homework tasks 'to learn' the vocabulary or spellings have been attempted.
- Labelling a diagram from memory on the basis of work completed at home.
- Recalling key facts, dates or people from memory on the basis of homework (or homework over a sequence of lessons).
- Hinge questions. Pupils are given a series of questions, essentially multiple-choice questions, on the board and are given a limited amount of time to answer. Hinge questions are a good way to ascertain whether the bulk of your class understood the homework set. Basically, they have multiple-choice questions that will act as a 'hinge point' by informing the teacher whether pupils are ready to move on (see Figure 6.2).

Quick Quiz - back of your books

1. Rainfall is a type of precipitation. Name two other types of precipitation.
2. Name one store of water in the water cycle.
3. What is hydraulic action?
4. What is condensation?
5. What type of erosion is like sandpaper?
6. What is attrition?
7. What does the term 'solution' mean in relation to river erosion?
8. What are the three types of weathering?
9. Name a river in Africa.
10. Name a river in Europe.

Figure 6.1 A quick book-based low-stakes quiz used in geography. The questions are checking homework on river erosion. These questions can be peer- or self-assessed (courtesy of Martyn Essery).

Designing low-stakes tests

The types of tests outlined above are very straightforward. However, despite this, question design is extremely important. Key aspects of sound question design to check homework would need to include the ideas listed on the following page.

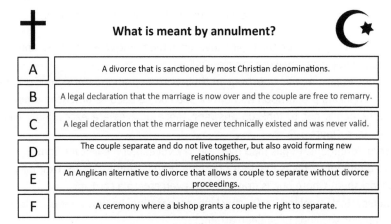

Figure 6.2 An example of a hinge question in religious education. This is part of three hinge questions checking a preparation homework on divorce and annulment. Pupils answer using mini-whiteboards.

- **An appropriate level of challenge.** Is the question pitched in a way that the pupil needs to think about the answer as opposed to immediately identify what is clearly correct (too easy) or take a complete guess (too hard)? Of course, a set of questions may involve a mixture of 'easy' and 'hard' questions – perhaps to build confidence in pupils – but if pupils do not need to think about the correct answer, it is questionable whether they are recalling information in a way that aids memory.
- **Ensure that you use plausible distractors.** In a similar vein to the above, if using multiple-choice tests, ask yourself whether the choices are realistic. If the distractors are obviously incorrect, what is the point of asking the question in the first place? Also, remember that pupils are at home and can look up information or ask someone, so consider whether your distractors require a certain amount of thought before answering.
- **Avoid ridiculous, obviously impossible and joke questions.** Research also suggests that we should avoid silly or joke questions as well those that are clearly nonsense. Essentially, these are not plausible distractors and the well-intentioned humour can distract from learning.
- **Additional areas of caution** of low-stakes testing, particularly multiple-choice tests, include questions that are
  - ○ irrelevant or too ambiguous for pupils to make sense of
  - ○ poorly worded or too complex to comprehend
  - ○ about right but on a different topic area.

Multiple-choice questions

Of course, all of the points above relate to multiple-choice questions. At TRFS and in my own practice, multiple-choice questions are used regularly, especially via the use of technology. In terms of both checking preparation homework and setting retrieval practice homework tasks, perhaps the easiest way to create a multiple-choice test is by using Google Forms/

Quizzes (see www.google.co.uk/forms/about), which has a quiz option. Google Forms also allows you to

- record scores
- identify areas for targeted or whole-class support
- add to trackers or spreadsheets (see Table 6.2 for an example, although, as low stakes, these should not be used for awarding current working grades).

Moreover, using Google Forms/Quizzes is relatively simple. All you need to do is

- head to forms.google.com
- click 'Settings' → 'Quizzes' → 'Make this a quiz'
- experiment with creating your own quiz.

Other options for making online quizzes include the following:

- Quizlet: www.quizlet.com
- Socrative: www.socrative.com
- Plickers: www.plickers.com
- Kahoot: www.kahoot.com

Again, although all of the above can be used for checking pupils' understanding of homework tasks, most can be used to set retrieval practice tasks as well. Practitioner Research Box 6.1 discusses the potential impact of low-stakes testing in language learning.

Table 6.2 A spreadsheet with Google low-stakes test scores (courtesy of Martyn Essery)

Class 8HU-B	Percentage correct	Water cycle	Journey	Corrosion	Transportation	Flooding	River chess	Trip prep	Final check
Number of questions		10	10	20	10	10	10	10	10
Class average	63%	5.8	6.4	11.9	6.8	7.1	7.3	5.1	6.5
Pupil 1	64%	4.5	7	15	8	6	6	5	6
Pupil 2	71%	9	6	14	6	7	7	6	9
Pupil 3	68%	4.5	3	18	7	8	8	5	8
Pupil 4	90%	10	9	20	8	9	10	6	9
Pupil 5	41%	6	4	12	5	2	2	2	4
Pupil 6	51%	5	5	9	3	8	8	4	4
Pupil 7	79%	7	8	19	9	8	8	6	6
Pupil 8	76%	6	7	11	10	9	9	7	9
Pupil 9	69%	6	5	12	6	9	9	5	10
Pupil 10	53%	6	6	16	Absent	7	Absent	7	6
Pupil 11	58%	8	7	4	7	10	10	2	4
Pupil 12	53%	3	9	11	5	6	6	3	5
Pupil 13	37%	4	7	4	5	5	5	3	Absent
Pupil 14	56%	4	8	7	5	9	10	4	3
Pupil 15	52%	3.5	5	10	8	7	7	3	3

Practitioner Research Box 6.1

Michael Shippey – Low-stakes testing in Spanish

Michael carried out some research that supports the findings of the Herts & Bucks Challenge Partners' Hub homework project as well as forming part of TRFS's development plan for 2019/20, which included low-stakes testing. As part of his National Professional Qualification in Middle Leadership (NPQML), Michael wanted to improve outcomes at Key Stage 4 in Spanish with an emphasis on prior middle attainers, essentially improving the department's General Certificate of Secondary Education (GCSE) grades at 7+. This was done through the following:

- embedding a consistent culture of low-stakes testing, which included both practice homework tasks online and preparation homework tasks for class tests, within the Spanish department
- revamping low-stakes tests in order to move away from a traditional-style vocabulary test to one that incorporates grammar and challenge questions
- increasing targeted engagement with online learning platforms such as Quizlet, which normally were completed at home as practice tasks

The project spanned two years and was specifically targeted at pupils moving from year 10 into year 11 in the top two sets in Spanish. Impressively, over a two-year period, the Spanish department at TRFS saw pupils' grades improve by a minimum of +0.72 per class on the contextually adjusted Progress 8 score between the baseline assessment data and final assessment data.

Michael is Head of Department for Spanish at TRFS. He was a member of the TRFS homework research group and continued to research the impact of low-stakes testing in the two years following the initial project.

Summative and formative assessment

When we discuss assessment, we often use two terms more than any other: *summative* and *formative*. Some teachers see one type as more useful than the other, but they should really be used in conjunction in order to give us as much information on the impact of our teaching in class as well as the homework tasks we set.

- Summative assessment simply measures the level of attainment that has been achieved in an end-of-unit test or exam. This would include a standard end-of-unit test, mock exam or even GCSE or AS/A-level exam.
- Formative assessment, on the other hand, places greater emphasis on feedback that can be applied by the pupil to improve their learning (not simply their grade). For instance, there will be plenty of diagnostic comments identifying pupils' strengths and weaknesses; often these comments come under the phrases 'what went well' and 'even better if'. Formative assessment should be continual throughout a course or scheme of work so that the pupil has constant feedback on how to improve.

What works best for homework? It goes without saying that using homework for summative assessment is fraught with undesirable difficulties. For example:

- pupils could cheat
- pupils might collaborate
- pupils might take longer than the designated time
- parents might help
- some pupils might not have a conducive home environment (i.e., no space to work or no chance of peace and quiet).

It might come as no surprise to say that homework is not really a tool for summative assessment. Any results will be dubious and have questionable accuracy. As Strandberg suggests, 'Research on how to assign and assess homework must consider the problems and conflicts that homework causes students, parents and teachers. Research is also needed to illuminate issues related to conditions for equity in relation to homework and feedback' (Strandberg, 2013, p. 325). However, it is worth noting that there is a gap in the research here as very few studies have looked at the grading and summative assessment of homework and those that have have shown very little evidence that summatively assessing homework has an impact on learning and achievement (Cooper, 2007). Some researchers feel that assessing homework can negatively impact pupils as the focus moves away from learning and towards attainment (Vatterott, 2009).

Nonetheless, there is still a strong case for formatively assessing homework. In one analysis, using data coming from standardised tests and questionnaires for teachers, pupils and parents, Murillo and Martinez-Garrido found that homework impacts learning and achievement if '(a) teachers handle homework, (b) these are reviewed and corrected in the classroom, and (c) students with lower performance have homework adapted to their needs' (2012, p. 157). This is also evident in studies suggesting that feedback on homework impacts learning and achievement. Some studies have shown that pupils like their homework assessed and graded, whereas others have suggested that pupils value homework more if it is assessed in some way, especially if it results in praise that they can show their parents (Peterson & Irving, 2008; Hallam & Rogers, 2018). Moreover, a wealth of evidence suggests that feedback, discussed below, has a positive impact on homework, learning and achievement. If this is so, surely some form of formative assessment or low-stakes testing is needed; this does not need to be graded summatively and can be qualitative as much as quantitative. Moreover, in class, summative assessments will still tell us how well pupils are doing and these are going to be affected by homework in some way.

Assessment for learning

As the curriculum has become more knowledge-based (as discussed in Chapter 4), it is important to use both class-based summative-based assessment and homework-based formative assessment to understand pupils' overall progress and whether our lessons and, indirectly, homework assignments are having any impact. Here, it is good to apply the ideas behind *assessment for learning*. The phrase assessment for learning (AfL) is one of the most used and emphasised in education today. It is primarily a form of formative assessment that advances pupils' understanding of the subject taught by giving *regular feedback* that informs them on how to improve on their current attainment or levels. The current popularity of the phrase can be traced to a paper by Black and Wiliam (2001), who define assessment as

> all those activities undertaken by teachers, and by their students in assessing themselves, which provide information to be used as feedback to modify the teaching and learning activities in which they are engaged. Such assessment becomes 'formative assessment' when the evidence is actually used to adapt the teaching work to meet the needs.
>
> (p. 2)

The key to understanding AfL is to see it as a diagnostic tool. Here, we can use AfL to gain knowledge of our pupils' academic progress, including their strengths and weaknesses as well as their interest in our subjects. We can also evaluate our own strengths and weaknesses by reviewing our pupils' work and plan interventions, re-teach topics or even request continuing professional development. Importantly, the key principle here is regular feedback, which must be useful to pupils; they must be able to comprehend any criticism given and understand how to improve. For instance, Haydn (2013, p. 418) suggests that AfL must incorporate these general principles (here, I will relate to homework in brackets and italics):

- providing helpful and constructive feedback to our pupils *(on homework practice tasks or work resulting from preparation tasks)*
- an inclusion of self- or peer-assessment (or both) at some stage in order to actively involve pupils in their learning *(this is easy; pupils essentially peer- and self-assess homework tasks when back in class)*
- a willingness to adjust our teaching through reflection on the outcomes of the assessments *(these can include homework tasks as well low-stakes tests that check homework tasks)*
- an awareness of pupil motivation and self-esteem in relation to assessment *(here, poor assessment in class could indicate a lack of preparation out of class)*
- lastly, sharing the success criteria with pupils *(this can inform practice and preparation tasks)*.

Subsequently, homework should occasionally be viewed by teachers to ensure that those pupils doing it properly get some decent qualitative feedback and guidance. Moreover, low-stakes tests can still give us a quantitative indication of our pupils' performance but one which we can take with a pinch of salt. Aside from that, we can assume from the majority of research so far that setting frequent homework tasks will impact summative assessments in class.

Marking and assessing homework

One of the bugbears of teachers everywhere is assessing work by marking it. I have spent days – no months – sitting at home marking, and the more homework I set, the more marking I used to have to do! However, there are ways to make marking, and therefore our ability to carry out formative assessment, easier. The first way is to use plenty of low-stakes tests and accumulate that data for evaluative (not grading) purposes. The second is to get pupils to peer- and self-assess – as mentioned earlier – so that they do the work for you. This can work well with engaged pupils but in some contexts is limited and means that you have not really had sight of your pupils' work. A third way, which I will champion here in relation to marking and formatively assessing homework, is *whole-class feedback*. I will then suggest an alternative method of marking homework, which can be used in schools that will not allow whole-class feedback.

Whole-class feedback

The irony of marking homework, especially in relation to formative assessment, is that it takes up loads of time – often when you are at home. In 2016, a Department for Education (DfE) working group found that the obsessive nature, depth and frequency of marking were impacting negatively on teachers' wellbeing and their ability to plan, prepare and deliver outstanding lessons. The working group put it this way:

> Marking has evolved into an unhelpful burden for teachers, when the time it takes is not repaid in a positive impact on pupils' progress... The consequence of this skewed dominance of written feedback means that teachers have less time to focus on the most important aspect of their job – teaching pupils.
>
> (DfE, 2016, p. 6)

Importantly, the working group suggested the need to refocus our energies on using assessment to inform our teaching as much as inform our senior leaders how great our marking is. I completely agree with this view. In previous roles, I have spent long periods of time *deep marking* and littering pupils' work with comments in red, green and purple pen in addition to filling in learning ladders and unit reviews. I have often done this not so much with my pupils in mind, but the senior leaders who might pick up pupils' books at any moment and go through their work to check that my marking conforms to school policy.

In response to this issue and concerns about teacher workload, colleagues of mine at TRFS conducted a series of trials around the time of the Herts & Bucks Challenge Partners' Hub homework project.[1] These trials built upon research into whole-class feedback and endeavoured to see whether they worked in our context. They did. This not only has revolutionised marking, assessment and feedback but also has allowed me to mark and formatively assess practice homework tasks in no time at all.

The mathematics of marking and assessing

Before I outline my school's procedures for whole-class feedback, consider this evidence from one teacher's experiences of implementing it.

- Initially, she had 120 books.
- She spent 5 minutes of marking time per book.
- She completed this four times per cycle.

- This is 2,400 minutes, or 40 hours, marking per cycle/term.
- It equates to 3.5 hours per week.
- This undeniably creates fatigue.

However, here's the alternative:

- She had 120 books.
- She spent 1.5 minutes per book.
- She completed four times per cycle.
- This is 720 minutes, or 12 hours, marking per cycle/term.
- This equates to 1 hour per week.
- This gives more time for the crucial element of planning teaching based upon the evidence from marking.

How does this work?

Whole-class feedback means that we do not actually 'put pen to paper' in pupils' books or on their homework but instead read through them making notes. These notes will look for trends and patterns, including common mistakes, misconceptions and areas for improvement as well as pupils' strengths. By assessing pupils' work, including any relevant homework tasks, as a class, whole-class feedback offers plenty of opportunity to demonstrate and model the different strengths and weaknesses as well trends in common spelling, grammar and punctuation (SPaG) mistakes (for an example of what this looks like, see Figures 6.3 and 6.4). Moreover, the feedback can identify ways to move grades up through tasks built on the back

Class	Teacher	Dates marked from and to (Cycle reference)
The code for your class	Pretty clear?!	Specific dates important so that pupils know the period they are looking at
Excellent work for celebration		**Common SPaG and numeracy mistakes/misconceptions**
Use this area to celebrate excellent work from your class This can be in relation to specific tasks, or general Highlight things such as excellent presentation, or marked improvement Use your knowledge of your class to decide whether naming pupils will work well or not		List the correct versions so that pupils can look for erroneous examples in their books Highlight grammatical errors too Ensure that you explain anything which might be misinterpreted or is unclear
Did you make any of these frequent mistakes or misconceptions?		**Which of these topics, skills, or content do you need to review?**
This is the place to record specific errors and misconceptions which arose frequently Specific issues in this box will require re-teaching if a significant number of the class have made the same mistakes		Here you record general issues which may have arisen frequently, such as if a task on a specific date was not completed by many pupils You may also record here is a technique or topic you have taught, and that you are confident pupils understand, was not used appropriately of referred to when required
Follow-up tasks - your teacher will guide you where to begin		
1. A clear list of tasks to complete here is essential 2. They will largely be based upon the feedback you have listed above and then explained in the feedback lesson 3. Tasks should be clear enough that pupils do not need your direction to work through the list 4. Some pupils may be able to miss the first task or two and start further down the list 5. It is worthwhile including an extension task at the end which challenges those who have completed all the feedback tasks required		

Figure 6.3 A template sheet (to be printed on green paper) with explanations for whole-class feedback (courtesy of Martyn Essery)

Class	Teacher	Dates marked from and to (Cycle reference)
10GG2	Mr Essery	10/2/18 - 9/3/18 (Spring Cycle 3)
Excellent work for celebration		**Common SPaG and numeracy mistakes/misconceptions**
SH - revision notes (on the wrong topic!) LSW, OT - answer to Q10 RW - exceptional revision notes, answers to 9-mark Qs JS, NB, EDV, JD - answer to Q11		less/fewer - use 'less' when the amount is not defined in units (eg. "the glass had less water in it") and use fewer when you are talking about a specific number (eg. "there were fewer than 200 jobs in the sector") receive
Did you make any of these frequent mistakes or misconceptions?		**Which of these topics, skills, or content do you need to review?**
'no of jobs' means 'number of jobs' - some people thought it meant 'no jobs' Explain the graph, don't just describe it Use statistics from the graph to illustrate your points Explore the negative aspects of the regeneration of the lower Lea Valley		Writing a conclusion to an evaluation question Complete the 9-mark question on effectiveness of an urban regeneration project (hands planning sheet) Use SEE to explore impact of human geography - social, economic, environmental Ensure that if you make a point about an advantage or disadvantage you follow up with analysis answering the question 'so what?'
Follow-up tasks - your teacher will guide you where to begin		
1. Review the guidance above and make purple pen corrections/improvements to your assessment 2. Tally up your multiple choice score and your written answers score to give a total out of 25 - share this total with Mr Essery 3. Review your book to complete any further purple pen corrections/completion of work 4. Begin considering the opportunities and risks of our visit to the Olympic Park on 21st March		

Figure 6.4 A completed sheet could look like this exemplar (courtesy of Martyn Essery)

of the feedback. Here, the feedback can be far more meaningful and purposeful in terms of active learning and thinking. The feedback is delivered in a lesson called DIRT (dedicated improvement and reflection time), which happens every three weeks in line with the school marking policy. The exact process for this is explained here:

1. Collect in a class set of books for marking.
2. Get a blank 'whole-class feedback' sheet ready (electronic or not).
3. Read through each book, making notes as to what you are finding on the sheet (remember, there is no need to write anything in pupil books).
4. Devise a set of feedback tasks and add these to the bottom of the sheet.
5. Print the feedback sheet off for each pupil (on green paper).
6. Plan a feedback task/lesson, giving pupils the time and means by which to act upon your feedback.

The importance of the feedback sheet and lesson in relation to homework

Compared with the research linking homework and assessment, which is mixed, the correlation between homework and feedback's impact on learning and achievement is far stronger. According to Hallam and Rogers (2018), research generally shows a consensus that monitoring, marking and feeding back on homework make pupils take it more seriously. Moreover, Walberg and Paik (2000) argue that feedback is fundamental to making homework impactful on learning and achievement (see Box 6.1 as well). However, there is a caveat here: as Hallam and Rogers (2018) point out at some length, poor-quality feedback can be demotivating and have a negative effect on self-esteem. Many pupils struggle to understand feedback as well, which

---

Box 6.1

Reflections on whole-class feedback from Adam Baker, Assistant Headteacher at Parmiter's School, Watford

"Whole-class feedback can be a very powerful tool for both students and the teacher, sharing with the students feedback after review work (written down helps as they can then revisit this) enables students to remove misconceptions they might have had or didn't know they had and for the teacher, it enables them to spend their time feeding back in a far more exact and purposeful way!"

---

makes the feedback redundant. In a similar vein, Esner (2017) argues that one of the problems with the deep marking technique briefly referenced above is that individual comments end up being very generic, making a mockery of individualised assessment via marking in the first place. Pupils' books are swamped with comments like 'add more detail here' or 'explain this' but lack the relevant additional detail on how to follow through on these directions. Some of these 'off-the-cuff' generic comments can also be disheartening for pupils regardless of their teacher's intention. Here, MacBeath and Turner (1990) found that pupils did not always see teachers' comments as helpful. Some pupils surveyed in their study said that they were reluctant to let teachers see their mistakes or that they failed to understand the homework. MacBeath and Turner conclude, 'This suggests an inappropriate understanding of homework which ought to be discussed by teachers, pupils, and parents' (ibid., p. 62). I couldn't agree more.

Therefore, some of the time saved by assessing homework by marking books must be invested in planning quality feedback sheets and follow-up DIRT lessons instead. There is no point giving any sort of feedback to pupils on their homework unless they have an opportunity to act upon it. Therefore, the feedback sheet should give clear instructions on how to improve or avoid common mistakes. The feedback lesson should involve various activities that allow pupils to improve their work; this could include modelling additional answers on the basis of pupils' 'what went wells' and 'even better ifs', especially using some of the retrieval practice tasks discussed in earlier chapters. Planning *purposeful tasks* based on what you have learnt from your review of their homework is the lynchpin of this new approach.

An alternative to whole-class feedback

If your school still insists on individually assessing and marking work, including homework, you could still read through the pupils' work and add an individual response based on common mistakes or misconceptions as well strengths of that pupil's work. Perhaps develop a feedback sheet similar to the above for each pupil. However, to save time, select only certain homework tasks to review. In my own practice, I normally review books and select two substantial pieces of homework out of the six or so tasks set over that period. The others are peer-assessed. Here, all pieces are marked or assessed in some way. Furthermore, by selecting certain pieces, you could devote more quality 'pen-to-paper' time if your school still insists on marking the actual books or papers. It is worth noting that I still approach some A-level tasks this way, especially if they are lengthy essays.

Key takeaways from Chapter 6

- It is evident that homework needs to be monitored by teachers if it is to have any impact. Here, teachers can employ various strategies to check learning, from questioning to peer-assessment, in order to both check that homework is done and get some idea of how well it is understood.
- This element of checking is closely related to Rosenshine's idea of review and cannot be ignored as an aspect of best practice.
- If questioning pupils, be sure to use hands-down strategies and allow for thinking time.
- There is ample evidence that low-stakes testing – often associated with retrieval practice – is an impactful way to check learning and informally assess pupils' progress. It can clearly be used to check that preparation tasks have been completed and, in some instances, can be set as homework itself. There are plenty of online platforms to facilitate this in addition to old-fashioned worksheets.
- Formally assessing pupils, especially through summative assessments, is more complicated. Whilst setting exam-style questions and essays as homework tasks are good ways to practise skills and knowledge retrieval, summative assessments should take place in the classroom. That said, these assessments still give an indication of how our homework tasks – as part and parcel of our general practice – are impacting on learning and achievement.
- There is a place, however, for formatively assessing homework tasks, especially in analysing pupils' strengths and weaknesses and for preparing feedback. Most pupils will carry out their homework as instructed and – over time – assessment for learning can inform how well homework tasks are being carried out as well as give a road map for feedback.
- Whole-class feedback can make marking homework quicker and easier but must also be accompanied by lessons or activities that build on that feedback.

Note

1 My colleague Martyn Essery and I wrote up the findings of the whole-class feedback trials at our school for the Chartered College of Teaching's *My College: Windows Into the Classroom* website; see www.my.chartered.college.temp.link/2018/10/how-reduce-teacher-workload-quality-marking-whole-class-feedback.

Suggested further reading

Roediger, H. L. III, Putnam, A. L. & Smith, M. A. (2011). Ten Benefits of Testing and Their Applications to Educational Practice. In J. P. Mestre & B. H. Ross (Eds.), *The psychology of learning and motivation: Vol. 55. The psychology of learning and motivation: Cognition in education* (pp. 1–36). Cambridge, MA: Elsevier Academic Press.
This is essential reading for anyone interested in low-stakes testing as well as quizzing more generally. The authors use research to identify 10 key benefits of testing. Moreover, the benefits are linked to developments in retrieval practice as well as spaced distribution.

Christodoulou, D. (2019) Whole Class Feedback: Saviour or Fad? A three-part blog. Retrieved from: https://blog.nomoremarking.com/whole-class-feedback-saviour-or-fad-5c54c463a4d0 [1 July 2020] Christodoulou argues that whole-class feedback is a potential 'game changer' that can dramatically improve your pupils' understanding of the subject and your understanding of how they learn. She champions those teachers experimenting with whole-class feedback, especially as they share ideas – many of which are hyperlinked in her last blog.

7 Planning, spaced distribution and interleaving

Chapter overview

This chapter includes the importance of *planning* homework, the effects of *cognitive load* on homework and the role of *spaced distribution*, or the *spacing effect*, in planning homework. It goes on to suggest that when setting homework tasks, we should consider *interleaving*, or mixing up topics, in order to maximise the impact on long-term learning and achievement.

Planning is an essential component of teaching and learning and there is no reason why homework should not be part of our planning process. Although the Office for Standards in Education, Children's Services and Skills (Ofsted, 2019) *School Inspection Handbook* states that inspectors do not wish to see curriculum planning in any specific format, including lesson plans, our Teaching Standards still require us to produce well-planned lessons. Standard 4, for example, requires us to 'plan and teach well-structured lessons' and says we should 'set homework and plan other out-of-class activities to consolidate and extend the knowledge and understanding pupils have acquired' (DfE, 2013, p. 11). This standard corresponds to the emphasis placed on knowledge in our curriculum – highlighted in Chapter 4 – and means that we should apply the strategies discussed in Chapters 4 and 5 in order to 'consolidate and extend the knowledge and understanding pupils have acquired' effectively. It goes without saying that planning homework tasks must incorporate these ideas if the outcomes of those tasks are to have any impact on learning and achievement.

Similarly, the Educational Endowment Fund (EEF) *Teaching and Learning Toolkit* (2020a, 2020b) shows that in the most impactful examples of homework on learning and achievement, the tasks set are seen as an integral part of the learning rather than an 'add-on'. It was also shown that high-quality feedback on homework is a key factor, which was emphasised in the previous chapter. Subsequently, homework needs to be incorporated into units of learning and be considered as an integral part of our lesson planning; homework tasks must build on what has been taught or will be taught, and feedback on homework must be accounted for in medium-term plans. Here, we should ensure that homework tasks:

- are planned to follow on from learning in class, perhaps retrieving the knowledge or practicing the skills learnt
- prepare pupils for the following lesson in the sequence being taught
- do not simply finish work that should have been completed in class
- are not set for the sake of it.

However, homework is more multifaceted in terms of planning than the Teacher Standards would suggest. We saw in Chapter 2 that research demonstrates that homework has more impact if tasks are manageable in terms of time as well as level of difficulty. Pupils have busy lives outside of school and we need to be aware of the curvilinear amount of time that is optimal for learning; planning and setting too much homework can be as counterproductive as setting none. We should also remember that pupils are given homework in other subjects. This means that we need to plan homework not only as classroom teachers but also within departments and across the school. Ideally, departments and schools need to coordinate planning for homework across the curriculum as a whole.

Avoid bottlenecks: planning homework across the school

The EEF Toolkit shows that short focused homework tasks are most impactful at secondary level and a similar picture is true at primary level – so long as homework is set regularly. The Toolkit repeats the findings of other researchers in that the optimal time is between 1 and 2 hours per day – perhaps a little longer for older pupils; as we know, the impact of homework diminishes beyond that time frame. Although the Department for Education (DfE) and Ofsted do not require homework to be set, let alone tell us how much, previous guidance was largely in line with the academic research on homework. Table 7.1 shows what the Department for Employment and Education (DfEE) suggested in 1998.

It is clear that time is limited and rouge (or self-important) teachers who set their pupils' vast amounts of homework need to be kept in line. The issue with the above guidance is that it does not coordinate homework setting between subjects and teachers within the school. Therefore, the DfEE suggested that pupils should be given timetables (see Table 7.2). These need to be planned by senior leaders with input from teachers (and arguably pupils) to bring a sense of order.

However, teachers and pupils should be made aware of these timetables routinely at the beginning of the year. Guidance for teachers as well as pupils and parents should also be set out in the school's homework policy. For example, The Reach Free School states how much should be set in its policy (see Box 7.1).

At Key Stage 3 (KS3), pupils should be given no more than 30 minutes per subject; at KS4, no more than 1 hour. This not only allows for adequate retrieval practice or preparation tasks to be set but fits in with the EEF Toolkit's findings that homework tasks have more impact if tasks are short and focused. KS5 is more open but that is because pupils have – on average – three subjects and less contact time. My colleagues, therefore, will plan homework in line with this guidance to ensure that pupils can manage and complete their learning.

Table 7.1 Department for Employment and Education (1998) guidance on time allocation for homework

Year group	Time allocation	Subjects
Years 1 and 2	1 hour per week	Reading, spelling, other literacy work and number work
Years 3 and 4	1 hour 30 minutes per week	Literacy and numeracy as for years 1 and 2 and occasional tasks in other subjects
Years 5 and 6	30 minutes a day (up to 2 hours 30 minutes per week)	Regular weekly schedule with continued emphasis on literacy and numeracy but also ranging widely over the curriculum
Years 7 and 8	45 to 90 minutes a day (between 3 hours 45 minutes and 4 hours 30 minutes per week)	Not specified
Years 8 and 9	1 to 2 hours a day (between 5 to 10 hours per week)	Not specified
Years 10 and 11	1 hour 30 minutes to 2 hours 30 minutes a day (between 7 hours 30 minutes and 12 hours 30 minutes per week)	Not specified

Table 7.2 Timetable given to pupils

Homework timetable – 7J

	Monday	Tuesday	Wednesday	Thursday	Friday
English		Hand in			Set
Mathematics	Set periodically throughout the week, amount in line with other subjects				
Science		Set			Hand in
Spanish			Set		Hand in
Humanities	Hand in		Set		
Technology			Hand in	Set	
Creative arts	Set		Hand in		Hand in
Citizenship	Set as required by the project that pupils are working on				

Box 7.1

The Reach Free School's home learning policy, Section 6

6. Progression of Home Learning from Year 7 to Year 13

6.1 Year 7, 8 and 9 – Pupils will be set work for home learning for each subject once a week, allowing, in all subjects other than mathematics, at least two days for it to be completed before the scheduled hand-in day. Owing to the nature of mathematics, it is often expected to be returned the next day. Homework tasks should total around 30 minutes per subject, per week.

6.2 Years 10 and 11 – Pupils will be set work for home learning as deemed appropriate by subject teachers, in collaboration with pupils. This will be a minimum of one piece per week per subject, and normal submission deadlines will follow at least two days later. Homework tasks should total around one hour per subject, per week.

6.3 Post 16 – Pupils will be required to manage their own time and will be issued deadlines within which to complete their work. They will be responsible for their own workload and will be expected to apportion their own time to complete tasks to or ahead of deadline. Homework tasks should total around three hours per subject, per week.

Cognitive load and planning homework

In Chapter 4, we learnt that in order to remember things over time we need to embed, or rather encode, facts and concepts into a schema that can help us process all the information and knowledge received at any given time. Didau and Rose (2016) used the term 'chunks' to describe these encoded snippets of information. Importantly, if we cannot build and fit these chunks into schemata, we are in danger of being overloaded with information to such an extent that none of it sticks, so to speak. It is worth pausing to consider some of the research behind *cognitive load theory*, which should be a consideration when we both plan homework tasks and give out instructions to complete the tasks. Again, we know that pupils prefer homework that is manageable and, importantly, within reason in terms of ability and time.

P[L explain how cognitive load can be split into two types (although there are other types too). These are *intrinsic cognitive load* and *extrinsic cognitive load*. Both of these relate to homework.

- Intrinsic cognitive load refers to the nature of the task itself. What is important here is the availability of prior knowledge via a schema. Here, if we set too much homework that is not related to prior learning or previously taught content – as stressed throughout the previous chapter – then it will be harder for the pupils to either practice the tasks set for homework or take account of all the knowledge they have to prepare for an upcoming lesson.
- Extraneous cognitive load is extremely relevant to homework as it relates to both the conditions of learning as well as how the task itself is set. For instance, pupils will need to complete their homework in conditions laden with distractions, which may make focus on and attention to the tasks more difficult (but not desirable). Moreover, if we give out reams of instructions to pupils as well as copious amounts of information as a stimulus, to be interpreted or even as a scaffold, it could be counterproductive as pupils will not be able to take anything in.

This is important as any homework tasks set should be manageable. For instance, Rosenshine (2012) suggests that new content should be introduced in small steps with opportunities to practice after each step. Here, the tasks should be small but regular and fit well within the curvilinear limits discussed above. We also see that these ideas on cognitive load fit in with a lot of the research set out in Chapter 2, especially the issue of making sure that tasks are doable and do not overload pupils. Perhaps, when setting homework, we should do the following:

- Set homework with clear and concise instructions.
  - Ensure that instructions are not too ambiguous.
  - Ensure that instructions are not too long or complex.
- When setting, ensure that pupils are clear on how it relates to what they have learnt or will be learning.
- Pitch the homework within the boundaries of the pupils' abilities.
- Set tasks that can be completed within suggested time frames.
- Streamline tasks so that the homework is not disjointed.

- Make sure that guides or resources supporting pupils are adequate but not overburdening.
- Be specific with tasks like reading – give pupils page numbers or sections etc.
- Avoid limitless possibilities (i.e., 'research everything you can about space travel').

Basically, avoid setting too much or confusing the pupils. Some of the ideas outlined for setting preparation homework tasks in Chapter 5 overlap here.

Spaced distribution

In Chapter 4, we saw that retrieval practice is an essential tool for improving our long-term memory and consolidating schemata. It is also a powerful way of combating the so-called *forgetting curve*, which is a hypothesis on the decline of memory retention over time by German psychologist Hermann Ebbinghaus (see Figure 7.1). Although Ebbinghaus's own studies may be questioned by psychologists and scientists today because of his limited methodology, studies have replicated his ideas with positive results (see, for example, Murre & Dros, 2015).

The curve shows how information and knowledge are lost over time, especially when there is no attempt to retain them. This graph, typical of many illustrating the forgetting curve, highlights the tendency of our memory of newly learned knowledge to decrease by half in a matter of days or weeks unless we consciously and proactively review the learned material. Importantly, it is argued that memory can be enhanced through regular rehearsal and retrieval of information.

Subsequently, we should ideally be setting homework tasks, particularly those focused on retrieval practice, but also preparation for low-stakes testing, at regular spaced intervals. Researchers have demonstrated that the academic *mastery* of a subject requires regular and focused practice over time. Here, Marzano (2005) argues that after only four practice sessions pupils reach a halfway point to potentially mastering an area of study or cognitive skill. However, it would take more than 24 practice sessions before pupils reach 80% mastery in that topic or subject area. He also points out that this practice will happen over a span of days or weeks, depending on the time and frequency of sessions, and cannot be rushed. Similarly, Newell and Rosenbloom (1981, p. 47) suggest that the *chunking model* of learning provides a theory of knowledge acquisition that would improve memory over time, which fits

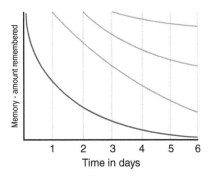

Figure 7.1 Ebbinghaus's forgetting curve (adapted from Wikicommons)

in nicely with our use of the terms chunking and schema. It is incumbent upon us, then, to set homework tasks on specific topics or areas of study as well as specific skills over longer periods than the area of study takes to cover in class; this will involve some element of planning too.

The benefits of regular practice are backed up by research on *spaced distribution*, also referred to as the *spacing effect*. Researchers have found that spacing practice massively improves knowledge retention over time – so long as the gap or space between activities is right. For instance, an experiment by Cepeda et al. had participants 'learning obscure facts through various combinations of spacing gaps, which included 0, 1, 2, 4, 7, 11, 14, 21, 35, 70, or 105 days, and test delays of 7, 35, 70, or 350 days' (2008, cited in Carpenter, 2014, p. 4). The researchers found that shorter spacing gaps were more conducive for short-term knowledge retention but that longer spacing gaps were more beneficial for longer-term retention. Importantly, Cooper (2007) also argued that practice tasks have more impact than preparation tasks if they are distributed, or spaced, over time. There is a clear link between impactful homework and spaced distribution here, and homework gives an opportunity to set knowledge retrieval tasks that are spaced over time without taking up lesson time that may need to be devoted to new material.

Interleaving homework tasks[1]

Please indulge me in an anecdote. I hated times tables with a passion when I was young. At first, I struggled and tended to find the overly repetitive rote memorisation of them an utterly miserable experience. I even stuck them on doors and by my bed to go over whilst sitting on the toilet or lying awake at night, until I became so sick of them. It was not too long before I just gave up; this must have been in year 5. It did not help that I had to occasionally stand up in class - perhaps this was my primary school teacher's way of checking learning - and recite them like a prayer. This was awful too. Eventually, the school sought extra help and sent me to some special educational needs (SEN) specialists at a place called the Independent Learning Centre, branded 'The ILC', or 'The Idiots' Learning Centre' to my peers. I occasionally get flashbacks of this. For instance, about four years ago, I went into a maths class as part of my 'Senior Leadership Team on tour' duty and the well-meaning maths teacher asked me what 6×7 is. I gave the wrong answer. I then panicked, thought about it, and gave another wrong answer. Everyone seemed embarrassed.

I was determined not to let my son, Anand, experience this. We practice times tables regularly at home - most evenings and for at least half an hour on Sunday afternoons. This had been going badly until my wife decided to intervene and inadvertently threw in some desirable difficulties that really helped him to get a better grip on his times tables. My mistake had been elementary; whereas my wife mixed the times tables up immediately after he had mastered each table in turn, I had been wasting time getting him to go over each times table in a rote fashion. Although my wife's method is in no way groundbreaking - most parents will do this and it is similar to most peoples' use of flash cards - it does demonstrate a very simple example of what is called *interleaving*. Her method became to recite them a number of times in order, mix up that order for the particular times tables and, lastly, mix them with other times tables. Despite the odd mistake, Anand now knows them and can recite without hesitation. This was how we adapted his times tables homework tasks (see Table 7.3).

Another example of this is spelling lists set as homework at primary school. If spellings are learnt in a sequence, then Anand will learn the spelling in context, simply reciting what comes next. When I started moving the order of his listed spellings, he initially found this harder but eventually got them right despite complaining. However, I also liked to throw in some previous spellings once he got the hang of it. This is both to combat the forgetting curb, discussed above, and to make it harder. Below is an example based on the *ay*, *a-e* and *ai* spelling pattern (see Table 7.4).

My son's headteacher, Claire Keilty, echoed this when we were discussing times tables. Her view, as a primary school teacher, is that the *rehearsal* of times tables does work. However, this rehearsal need not be done sat at a table via rote learning. She suggests that parents

Table 7.3 Interleaved times tables homework task for a year 4 pupil

7 times table in order	7 times table mixed up	Interleaved times tables
$1 \times 7 = 7$	$6 \times 7 = 42$	$9 \times 9 = 81$
$2 \times 7 = 14$	$10 \times 7 = 70$	$6 \times 4 = 24$
$3 \times 7 = 21$	$1 \times 7 = 7$	$2 \times 8 = 16$
$4 \times 7 = 28$	$5 \times 7 = 35$	$5 \times 5 = 25$
$5 \times 7 = 35$	$12 \times 7 = 84$	$7 \times 3 = 21$
$6 \times 7 = 42$	$7 \times 7 = 49$	$11 \times 6 = 66$
$7 \times 7 = 49$	$4 \times 7 = 28$	$4 \times 4 = 16$
$8 \times 7 = 56$	$11 \times 7 = 77$	$10 \times 12 = 120$
$9 \times 7 = 63$	$2 \times 7 = 14$	$8 \times 8 = 64$
$10 \times 7 = 70$	$9 \times 7 = 63$	$2 \times 2 = 4$
$11 \times 7 = 77$	$8 \times 7 = 56$	$12 \times 7 = 84$
$12 \times 7 = 84$	$3 \times 7 = 21$	$3 \times 3 = 9$

Table 7.4 Interleaved spellings homework task for a year 4 pupil

Weekly spellings	Weekly spellings mixed up	Some weekly spellings mixed with previous spelling lists
Betrayal	Acquaint	Terrain
Prevail	Remember	Sentence
Indicate	Prevail	Prevail
Ascertain	Indicate	Disarray
Imitate	Hesitate	Refrain
Translate	Sentence	Waylaid
Refrain	Imitate	Ascertain
Hesitate	Betrayal	Campaign
Constraint	Refrain	Acquaint
Acquaint	Translate	Betrayal
Remember	Ascertain	Hibernate
Sentence	Constraint	Hesitate

can teach times tables anywhere at any time. Whether before school, in the car or on a train on a day out, parents can simply ask their children to recite the times tables with them, or even better, randomly ask them what is 5 × 4 or 9 × 6, perhaps whilst waiting for food at a restaurant. This not only allows pupils to learn in a different context, as discussed briefly in Chapter 4, but also is an example of *spaced interleaving*.

Essentially, interleaving emphasises mixing pre-taught topics when planning spaced or distributed practice in order to facilitate deeper consideration of the knowledge being recalled. Basically, mixing up content boosts learning compared with more traditional methods of block learning where pupils master one topic before moving on to the next. Mixing up the content affects pupils in two ways, according to Pan (2015): the first way is that it improves the brain's ability to tell apart, or discriminate between, concepts; the second is that it strengthens memory associations between these concepts.

Moreover, interleaving can be combined with distributed practice and retrieval to create a number of *desirable difficulties* in one strategy. For example, purposely revisiting taught content and practicing relevant problems in activities that are distributed or spaced over time (for example, A1... A2... A3) results in better knowledge retention, especially in terms of long-term memory, than if the lessons or activities are blocked together or limited to a closed sequence of lessons where no other content gets revisited or reviewed (for instance, A1A2A3) (MIT, n.d.). Here, instructors at the Massachusetts Institute of Technology (MIT) suggest teaching subject knowledge and skills in an interleaved fashion so that a task related to one aspect of a previously taught unit of learning or topic area is followed by a different task related to a different aspect of a previously taught unit of learning or topic area (as in A1B1C1B2C2A2C3A3B3). This has been found to have higher learning gains than simply practicing tasks grouped by types (for example, A1A2A3B1B2B3C1C2C3). Furthermore, combing spaced practice with interleaved subject content adds a number of key learning strategies together (Shatz, n.d.). These include the following:

- **Forgetting.** Studies suggest that a little forgetting is good for retrieval practice as the mind has to work harder to recall information. By mixing old topics with newish ones, the mind will need to retrieve knowledge that is close to being lost (Bjork & Bjork, 2019a, 2019b).
- **Desirable difficulties.** Interleaving is seen as aiding the retrieval of information as mixing topics up creates a desirable difficulty, which forces the brain to work harder and improve retrieval, especially in terms of long-term memory (Bjork & Bjork, 2011; see also Birnbaum, Kornell, Bjork & Bjork, 2012).
- **Contextual interference.** This is another mechanism for improving the retrieval of information from the long-term memory; the pupil has to identify between various concepts, especially those that might be similar (Rau et al., 2010).
- **Elaborative rehearsal.** This is where pupils focus on remembering the meaning of items that they are memorising, instead of focusing on simply repeating those items verbatim, which is more conducive if retrieved knowledge is interleaved as it involves greater mental effort to distinguish the correct answers (Shea & Morgan, 1979).

Therefore, in terms of planning learning, interleaving is the opposite of blocked learning, which means that pupils learn each topic in turn as opposed to 'mixing up' the subjects.

Lots of specific studies look at interleaving, which I will not go over here, but Bjork and Bjork (2019b) offer a good exposition for anyone interested. However, it is worth mentioning the work of Rohrer (2012), who has shown that whilst pupils using blocked practice were able to recall subject content more accurately in their immediate lesson (or learning), pupils who used interleaved practice were better at recalling subject content the next day. Moreover, Rohrer found that interleaving helped pupils distinguish between information taught, especially when that information was similar; this avoided pupil confusion between concepts or terms when retrieving knowledge. For example, pupils often mistake words with similar spellings, such as 'allusion' and 'illusion', or confuse strategies when problem solving, including in mathematics.

Interleaving: having an impact on maths homework

Rohrer and his colleagues were the first to research interleaving in actual schools; their study on pupils learning about geometry and algebra involved homework and testing as interleaved practice (Rohrer et al., 2015). This study looked at the teaching of algebra and geometry over 3 months in three middle schools in Tampa, Florida. Here, the pupils' weekly lessons were largely unchanged from their usual practice. However, weekly homework worksheets featured either interleaved or blocked tasks. Five of the nine classes in the study used interleaving for slope problems and blocking for graph problems; the reverse occurred in the remaining four. After the sequence of homework tasks, a review lesson was held 5 days later before surprise tests one day or one month later. The researchers found that when the test was one day later, scores were 25% better for problems studied via interleaving; at one month later, the interleaving advantage grew to 76%. Although this study focused on maths, other researchers suggest that a way to establish effective interleaving might be to plan into current lessons activities that briefly review previously learned information. These reviews could also be implemented as homework tasks, which may be particularly advantageous when class time is limited (see, for example, Carpenter, 2014).

Interleaving: having an impact on religious education homework?

As part of a wider Herts & Bucks Challenge Partners' Hub research project, following on our initial homework project (see Chapters 1 and 3), I have been using interleaved homework tasks in addition to interleaved starter questions in my General Certificate of Secondary Education (GCSE) religious education (RE) classes. Although the overall impact is hard to measure – as I am using various interventions – my classes have met with relative success since interleaving has been applied. Basically, each week my lessons consist of the following:

- Six starter questions that are given at the start of each lesson that week: three on the current topic, two on a previous topic and a last one on another previous topic.
- Three homework questions that are set once that week: one on the current topic and two on previous topics.

- The three homework questions included 4- or 5-mark questions; these take about five minutes each; so in a 30-minute homework, pupils have no more than 15 minutes of writing time with at least 15 minutes of preparation time if they want it.
- These interleaved tasks are distributed/spaced out as in Table 7.5.

In addition to the above, pupils are cyclically assessed on previously taught content. Within a six- or seven-week half term, all my GCSE classes will sit at least two timed assessments in exam conditions and – with the exception of formal mocks – will have two sections from the GCSE syllabus; these include the current topic taught and a previously taught unit. The latter is planned in a sequence to ensure that pupils are assessed proportionally in terms of the course's overall content. This combination of interleaved starters, homework and assessments seems to be working: my 2018 GCSE cohort attained a Progress 8 score of 1.72, which suggests that they achieve higher than their estimated grade by at least 1.72 grades. My 2019 cohort's Centre Assessed Grades also showed a Progress 8 score over a grade higher than the pupils' estimated grades. It is worth noting that some of the responses in the Hub research project included pupils from these classes; they seemed to approve of this strategy. Of course, I have no direct evidence that interleaving has impacted on these scores – it could well be the simple use of retrieval or spaced practice as well as other interventions.

Table 7.5 Year 11 religious education (RE) General Certificate of Secondary Education (GCSE) interleaved starter and homework questions

Week	Starter questions 1 to 3	Starter questions 3 and 4	Starter question 6	Homework 1	Homework 2	Homework 3
1	Current topic	Christian beliefs	Religion & life	Current topic	Islamic beliefs	Religion & life
2	Current topic	Christian practices	Religion & crime	Current topic	Islamic practices	Religion & crime
3	Current topic	Islamic beliefs	Relationships & families	Current topic	Religion & life	Relationships & families
4	Current topic	Islamic practices	Christian beliefs	Current topic	Religion & crime	Christian beliefs
5	Current topic	Religion & life	Christian practices	Current topic	Relationships & families	Christian practices
6	Current topic	Religion & crime	Islamic beliefs	Current topic	Christian beliefs	Islamic beliefs
7	Current topic	Relationships & families	Islamic practices	Current topic	Christian practices	Islamic practices

Limitations of spaced distribution and interleaving

Despite swearing by these ideas, I am appreciative that some people might raise some concerns in how teachers apply these strategies in practice. One of the biggest issues, for example, with the research on spacing is whether spacing should be equally distributed or expanded (in that intervals expand over time). Although evidence exists for the latter, it is contested (see, for example, Balota, Duchek & Logan, 2007). This might seem a relatively minor academic disagreement, but if we are to adapt these ideas wholesale into our classrooms and schools, we do need to be wary of how our evolving understanding of learning may change. Also, Karpicke and Bauernschmidt (2011) have suggested that more investigation needs to be carried out on how intervals are calculated, the effects of different procedures in implementation and the longer-term effects of spacing on pupils' learning and achievement. Many of these studies are short-term and completed with adults on obscure topics. In a practical sense, I also understand that what I am advocating – as best practice – could involve hours of planning and also not necessarily be conducive to every context, subject or pupil.

In relation to interleaving, Firth (2018) suggests that we need to be cautious of research as studies often include limited sample sizes and bypass the diversity of learners we find in our classrooms, which is certainly true of a lot of evidence cited above. Firth also calls for more research into how the negative short-term classroom effects of interleaving and spacing, such as cognitive load, are adequately counteracted by improved long-term ability to retrieve information and skills. Indeed, so far, researchers have mostly investigated the impact of interleaving in short-term studies, but it would be useful to see the impact over longer timescales, perhaps facilitated with longitudinal studies or pupils in actual schools.

Key takeaways from Chapter 7

- It is essential that we plan homework tasks. This is threefold in that we must plan appropriate tasks (see Chapters 3, 4 and 5, for example), we must be considerate of pupils' time at home and the curvilinear impact on learning and, lastly, we need to be aware of issues of cognitive load.
- It is important, therefore, that every couple of years teachers have In-Service Education and Training (INSET) on planning homework and be regularly reminded of school policies and timetables. It goes without saying that planning homework should be included in teacher training courses; it is a Teacher Standard after all.
- Any plans should account for cognitive load. We all talk about work/life balance and this is no different for our pupils. Chapter 2 told us that pupils studied by homework researchers like their homework to be challenging yet doable and manageable and we must bear this in mind; keep instructions clear and concise and avoid ambiguous tasks. Differentiate tasks if needs be, but make sure that the tasks are pitched at the right level in general.
- Research on spaced distribution and interleaving is compelling and we should not ignore this in our practice, even if incorporating it looks overly complicated. As discussed in Chapter 4, pupils need to know an awful lot to pass their exams and increase their life chances. If spaced distribution and interleaving, alongside retrieval practice and low-stakes testing, can combat the forgetting curve, we have a duty to plan these strategies into our lessons, homework tasks, schemes of learning and overall practice.

Note

1 Interleaving formed part of a Herts & Bucks Challenge Partners' Hub project following on from the retrieval practice and homework projects. I presented our findings at the 2020 UKEdChat Conference and blogged about them at www.mrjoneswhiteboard.blog. This, in turn, was reposted on the *UKEdChat blog*; see www.ukedchat.com/2020/04/04/interleaving-practice/.

Suggested further reading

Bjork, R. A. & Bjork, E. L. (2019). *The Myth that Blocking One's Study or Practice by Topic or Skill Enhances Learning*. In C. Barton (Ed.), *Education Myths: An Evidence-Informed Guide for Teachers*. Woodbridge, UK: John Catt Publishing.
Elizabeth and Robert Bjork have been researching the science of learning for years and have a wealth of knowledge to share with teachers. In this chapter, they look at interleaving and give a readable and concise overview of the current research on interleaving, including brief descriptions of various studies. They make the case for interleaving over blocked learning.
Carpenter, S.K. & Agarwal, P.K. (2020). *How to Use Retrieval Practice to Boost Learning: Spacing*. Retrieved from: https://www.retrievalpractice.org/about [9 June 2020].
Shana Carpenter and Pooja Agarwal have written this short but informative guide to spacing. It is worth reading as many teacher-oriented books only briefly cover spacing, but this booklet covers it in more depth. It is well explained and covers what types of learning benefit from spacing, how spacing works as well as possible questions addressing practical issues.

8 Supporting pupils and parents

Chapter overview

This chapter starts with a discussion on pupils' views on homework and then looks at how we can support pupils in school and at home; this includes the use of homework clubs, rewards, sanctions and technology. The chapter also looks at issues facing pupils with special educational needs before looking at how we can support parental involvement with homework.

Pupils' views of homework: it's not all bad!

Despite my teenage angst over homework and the consistent chasing of particular pupils for homework in my current roles, pupils in the UK and US overall believe that *homework helps* them to do well in school and impacts on achievement; some even say they often learn a lot from it (Black 1990; Keys, Harris & Fernandes, 1997; MacBeath and Turner 1990; all cited in Hallam, 2004 and Hallam & Rogers, 2018). This rather positive attitude surprised me, but digging deeper, I found that a study carried out in 1941 seemed to suggest the same thing: of 115 elementary (primary) pupils and 86 high school (secondary) pupils surveyed, 69% of the high school pupils preferred receiving homework to not receiving it and 77% of the elementary pupils saw the importance of homework; only 31% of the high school pupils wanted no homework at all (Ambuehl, 1941). Interestingly, as suggested in previous chapters, pupils preferred homework in reasonable amounts.

MacBeath and Turner (1990) found that the majority of the 1,011 pupils they surveyed said that they 'enjoyed homework' at least sometimes but 26% of primary pupils and 30% secondary pupils reported that they 'never enjoyed it' (MacBeath and Turner, 1990, p. 18). The biggest complaints in this study were that homework prevents pupils from doing other things and that it can take too long, which reinforces the idea of moderating the amount time spent on homework. MacBeath and Turner suggest that pupils are most likely to value homework when:

- it is well explained
- they are given advance notice and have adequate time to do it
- it is at their level of ability
- it is interesting or varied.

Quite simply, the first aspect of supporting pupils is getting the above right. This combines the advice in previous chapters, especially on setting homework clearly and planning it to avoid overloading pupils on certain days. MacBeath and Turner also found that pupils are more likely to be motivated to attempt homework and that the impact will be greater in situations where teachers and the school monitor homework and provide additional support to pupils, especially those with special educational needs or other social difficulties. Monitoring and feedback were emphasised in Chapter 6 but are worth mentioning again. Help, monitoring and feedback with homework are clearly essential as other researchers find that '[p]upils often report that homework has little relationship to the work in hand, it is poorly set, marked late, and that there is a lack of pupil-teacher interaction resulting in poor feedback' (Hallam, 2004).

Supporting pupils in school

There is plenty of evidence that not every pupil has an ideal *learning environment* at home. Moreover, some pupils – from time to time – suffer setbacks or face obstacles in completing homework. These can be relatively straightforward, such as a pupil moving home or being ill, to more complicated, perhaps they share a room with siblings, and to the frustrating – they have fallen out with their boyfriend or girlfriend and were too lovelorn to put pen to paper. To support pupils facing these issues, schools and departments can offer some of the ideas listed below.

- **Homework clubs**. These can take place at lunchtime or after school if teachers are around to staff them. Importantly, for these to be effective, the clubs should be staffed by a variety of teachers who can help pupils with specific homework tasks.
- **Department homework clubs**. These allow for more precise targeted support for pupils as the staff on hand are subject specialists. The only issue here is that you could end up with too many clubs and confusion about which to attend.
- **Departmental 'catch-up' sessions**. The humanities department at The Reach Free School set up a 'catch-up' session for incomplete homework on Thursday lunchtimes. This was staffed by humanities specialists on a termly rota but was not quite a club as pupils with a reluctance to complete homework were directed to attend (not quite a 'detention' in terms of semiotics!).
- **Curriculum time**. Although curriculum time is precious, The Reach Free School timetables one session a week for pupils in Key Stage 3 (KS3) and two sessions a week at KS4 for pupils to complete particularly difficult homework tasks or collaborate on tasks if necessary. All pupils in a certain year group have their session at the same time and teachers from most subjects, and always maths, English, and science, are circulating to help pupils with particularly challenging tasks.

There are quite a few studies on the impact of homework clubs and the findings seem to suggest that they can have an impact on learning and achievement if run well and qualified staff are involved (Hallam & Rogers, 2018). Inevitably, evidence suggests that unsupervised or less focused clubs have little impact.

Supporting pupils at home

This is trickier as we do not want to visit our pupils at 8 o'clock in the evening to help them understand Shakespeare's sonnets. Nonetheless, there are things we can do aside from the recommendations on tasks, setting instructions and planning already discussed in previous lessons.

- **Know your pupils**. Although you cannot possibly know everything about your pupils' homelife, and safeguarding processes mean you will not be party to everything affecting their lives, it is worth getting a sense of their home learning environment. Speak to your pastoral leads.
- **Create a 'homework culture' amongst your pupils**. Czerniawski and Kidd (2013) suggest discussing the best times and places to complete homework with pupils, encouraging the use of timetables and planners or online task trackers.
- **Ensure that pupils have access to task instructions**. Either provide planners or use an online platform that organises assignments. Planners might seem old-school, but there is evidence asserting their effectiveness (MacBeath & Turner, 1990; Baker, 2007).
- **Ensure that pupils have the correct resources**. Be realistic: can pupils adequately research your preparation task or practice the musical composition at home?
- **Access to technology**. If using technology, ensure that pupils all have access to a reliable device and the internet.

Rewards and sanctions

Ensure that you give praise and reward pupils for *quality homework*. Although this will be relative to the pupils' ability, the work completed will need to be rewarded for its content and not just because pupils have completed it. There are plenty of carrots here:

- positive comments and feedback
- shout-outs in class
- awarding points, such as 'credits', 'merits' or 'house points'
- prizes
- positive emails or calls home.

As well as sticks:

- taking away 'credits', 'merits' or 'house points'
- detentions, especially when work is incomplete
- emails or calls home to inform parents of non-completion
- homework reports.

However, it is worth leading with the carrot here as Payne (2015) has found that, in UK schools, sanctions such as losing break or lunchtime, or afterschool detentions, are often counterproductive in encouraging pupils to complete work, including homework. That said, positive contact with home was seen as more impactful in incentivising pupils to work hard. Other researchers suggest that both rewards and sanctions have their place, but really we should be establishing good behaviours as a simple *social norm* as opposed to something that needs to be overly enforced with extrinsic rewards and sanctions (Rose, 2017); homework is no different here. I would, nonetheless, set detentions for non-completion – so long as you insist that pupils complete the work. Explain its importance and help them if necessary.

Using technology to support pupils with homework

There are various online platforms and tools to support pupils with homework. Some common examples are Google Classroom, Show My Homework (Satchel) and Doddle. Many teachers are also starting to use applications like Screncatsify and Loom to make videos to support homework. These are particularly useful for giving additional instructions or modelling tasks. My own school uses Google and we integrate various homework tasks with relevant resources, such as combining videos (YouTube is part of Google and works seamlessly), lesson slides for recapping and worksheets that 'make a copy' for the pupils when they click on it; these then wait for us online to review and grade – Google can even put the grades in a spreadsheet for us! Here are the addresses to the aforementioned online platforms and applications:

- www.classroom.google.com
- www.teamsatchel.com
- www.doddlelearn.co.uk
- www.screencastify.com
- www.loom.com

There are also the online quiz websites named in previous chapters, such as Quizlet and Kahoot, as well subject-specific sites, like Times Tables Rock Stars. Other useful websites include BBC Bitesize and the Oak National Academy (see www.bbc.co.uk/bitesize and www. thenational.academy respectively).

Obviously, some general housekeeping rules should be abided by in order to facilitate good use of technology when setting homework tasks or using technology for homework. For instance, we should endeavour to do the following:

- Create a supportive atmosphere in all our tasks and communications with pupils. Do not expect pupils to be equally savvy in terms of technology. They might also still need help despite your amazing video explaining equilateral triangles.
- Be aware that setting homework online is still helped by routines. Consistency in the way in which we set and present work online is essential.
- Accept that any virtual learning environment, Google Classroom or other application is our virtual classroom. Explain our expectations with regard to layout of work, if completed online, and conduct on our comments stream/feed.

- Be realistic about what we want pupils to achieve. Consider the differing abilities in our classes or pupils; remember that technology does not necessarily make learning at home easier.
- If possible, use praise to motivate. In public on our videos and stream/feed for the whole class and in private comments on Google Classroom/your virtual learning environment for individuals.
- Consider those in our classes who are disadvantaged. Not everyone will have a printer or all the stationery we might expect them to have.
- If pupils can contact us at any time, we might want to specify times when they can.

Evidence on computer-assisted homework and technology is limited and invariably goes out of date pretty quickly. Also, this book has been written during the Covid-19 pandemic, meaning that teachers', pupils' and parents' use of technology for learning at home has undoubtedly accelerated. Here, we have to constantly adapt as technology changes society as well as the way we learn (Prensky, 2001). In their overview, Hallam and Rogers (2018) found that computer-assisted learning was useful where immediate answers and feedback can be given, which is now so easy with applications like Google Forms/Quizzes. They also cited evidence of chatrooms helping pupils engage with their learning. This is something my colleague Faye Caldwell has used to great effect. Some pupils studying literature were more likely to engage in their Google Classroom chatroom/feed than in class (see Practitioner Research Box 8.1).

Practitioner Research Box 8.1

Faye Caldwell – Using Google Classroom to stretch and develop pupils' intellectual curiosity

Many pupils lack the confidence in voicing their ideas before the class verbally. Using Google Classroom in this way allows pupils to express their ideas in a way that feels less formal, encouraging them to be more experimental and take risks. It is also a useful homework assignment as pupils can respond via Google at home and after the lesson. Generally, the most confident pupils will respond to the task more quickly, allowing pupils who are struggling to see a bank of 'model' responses to help their own thought process. During discussion activities within the classroom, the teacher may have time to ask only three or four pupils to share their ideas, but Google Classroom allows the teacher to formatively assess all of the pupils quickly, ensuring that every pupil contributes and is heard. The bank of responses from pupils can be used later by pupils for revision purposes or to generate an individual piece of extensive writing. Pupil feedback has been overwhelmingly positive – pupils have said that they enjoy the less formal way of expressing ideas and that they really feel like they are learning from one another in the process.

Pupil feedback

Pupil feedback has been extremely positive. Please read through some of the selected quotes below:

- 'Other peoples' comments help me to broaden my vocabulary' – Iris
- 'If you are a bit stuck you can look at the class comments and see what other people have written' – Wiktoria
- 'If you are struggling or are finding the tasks hard then there is always someone who understands and you can see their feedback' – Annabel
- 'People can see each other's comments therefore learning from each other as well as you teaching us' – Eoin
- 'Homework on Google Classroom helps and inspires me to explore what we are doing even more' – Megan
- 'It allows me to see how other people have interpreted the same text in different ways, giving me different ideas based on the same thing' – Esmeralda
- 'Google Classroom has helped me learn because we have the ability to see people's thoughts and answers straight away' – Liena
- 'Their ideas give me new ideas' – Esa
- 'I find it easier than sharing my ideas in front of a whole class' – Millie

Faye completed this as part of her contribution to the Challenge Partners' Hub homework project.

Supporting pupils of differing abilities

In recent decades, teachers have been encouraged to personalise learning, differentiate and – most recently – consider stretch-and-challenge activities for higher prior attainers (also known as 'more able' pupils). We are always being told to read special educational needs plans and be aware of Education, Health and Care Plans in order to facilitate greater inclusion in our classrooms. Indeed, this has been reflected in some studies on homework, especially when pupils have some common difficulties in learning that impacts on homework completion; these difficulties may include general cognitive development as well specific deficits in memory, attention, retrieval and information expression (Epstein et al., 1993; Hartjes, 2011). All of these difficulties can affect concentration, which has been shown to have a positive correlation with homework and achievement (Trautwein et al., 2006). Therefore, Hartjes argues, 'It follows that students with disabilities have lower expectancy and thus lower levels of homework concentration and completion' (2011, p. 82). Importantly, this could also affect pupils with emotional needs, including behavioural and attachment issues (see Katz, Kaplan & Gueta, 2009, for example).

In an overview of research on learning needs and homework, Hartjes (2011) found that the most common homework support strategies that have been shown to be impactful for pupils with learning needs, particularly disabilities, include the following:

- graphing of homework completion rates on charts
- providing extrinsic motivation and reinforcements for pupils
- the use of homework planning ideas or resources

- teaching pupils to use a self-monitoring system
- providing real-life tasks to foster interest
- allowing pupils to work in cooperative groups to complete assignments
- encouraging family involvement in homework.

However, despite the popularity of study skills programmes, self-monitoring and extrinsic motivation in schools, Hartjes, like many researchers, suggests a need for further research into the impact of these on achievement as well as pupils' wellbeing.

Although it may seem common sense to individualise or differentiate homework (see Vatterott, 2009 here), some studies suggest caution. If we take the common sociological concept of *labelling*, some researchers have found that labelling pupils as 'lower ability' can have detrimental effects on self-esteem and eventually achievement (Hargreaves et al., 1975). In relation to homework, Nelson et al. (1998) have reported that differentiated homework can have a negative impact on lower-ability pupils. This is particularly problematic if not dealt with in primary school as by the time pupils reach secondary school they can be completely demoralised in terms of academic ability (Witzel & Mercer, 2003). Hallam and Rogers (2018) suggest that grouping is relevant here, especially as differentiated homework is less common in mixed-ability classes than lower-ability ones.

Lastly, some studies have shown that more-able pupils benefit more from additional homework (Neilson 2005; Eren & Henderson, 2011). Research also suggests that higher-ability pupils are given more homework anyway (Hallam, 2004, Hallam & Rogers, 2018), which may suggest that teachers' perceptions of ability influence the amount and frequency of homework given to pupils. This is perhaps one area where optional extension tasks can be encouraged on top of the main homework tasks set. However, cognitive load and overwork apply to the more-able pupils as much as anyone else.

Parents' views of homework

According to research carried out in 2019 by the home tutoring group Oxford Home Schooling, parents are not too keen on homework. In their survey of 1,000 parents, 23% reported feeling under pressure when their children requested help whilst 31% were embarrassed if they could not help. Sadly, only 33% of parents felt confident helping their children with homework (Dorking, 2019). These statistics are not reflective of a new phenomenon as previous studies have indicated similar issues. Solomon et al. (2002) researched parental attitudes towards homework in Rochdale, near Manchester, and found that only 31% of parents were confident in the support they gave their children. This is important because some researchers argue that parents' attitudes towards homework directly impact on their children's attitudes towards it (Bempechat, 2004; Cooper et al., 1998; both cited in Blazer, 2009). Epstein and Van Voorhis (2001) state that pupils exposed to negative parental views on homework are far more likely to adopt these themselves; this can affect achievement as well as lead to conflict within school. This has led Hoover-Dempsey et al. to state, 'The most critical outcomes associated with parental involvement in homework may be found in the attitudes, ideas, and behaviors enacted by students in the course of school learning' (2001, p. 204). Although these studies – the Oxford Home

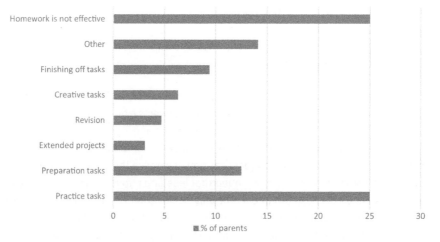

Figure 8.1 Parents' views of the most impactful types of homework as a percentage of tasks chosen by respondents (Herts & Bucks Challenges Partners' Hub)

Schooling research and the study in Rochdale – do not necessarily reflect antagonistic attitudes towards homework, any apathy or avoidance by parents will arguably have a knock-on effect on their children, too.

During the Challenge Partners' Hub research project, we also canvassed the views and opinions of 64 parents. Although most parents were supportive of homework being set, their overall views of homework were startlingly different from the rest of the Hub's research. For instance, only 14% saw practice assignments as being the most effective form of homework task; 25% of parents also said that no form of task is effective (see Figure 8.1). Parents, therefore, might appreciate an understanding of our rationale for setting the homework tasks we do as well as advice on how to support pupils with this. Their views were discussed in more detail in Appendix 3.

Supporting parents with their child's homework

Some researchers have found that for many parents, homework is 'invested with the opportunity for reparation for their own failures at school or other lost opportunities. Others felt that they lacked the competence to help and were disenfranchised by homework demands' (Solomon et al., 2002, p. 603). This suggests that effective communication is needed to build trust and support between parents and the school. Some practical strategies to support parents' engagement with homework can include the following:

- having a clear and parent-friendly homework policy
- sharing pupil homework timetables with parents
- ensuring that parents have access to homework planners or online homework websites

- if you use online websites (such as Google Classroom), offering training sessions or creating YouTube videos explaining how these work
- sharing curriculum plans with parents which reference to possible homework tasks
- offering documents that explain how parents can help their children with homework (make these available on your school website)
- offering training to parents on how they can support their children with homework, including maths and grammar sessions at primary level.

However, it would be wrong – looking at the research – to be overly negative about parents' attitudes or fears of homework. For instance, the Office for Standards in Education, Children's Services and Skills (Ofsted) (2017) claims that the majority of parents they survey say homework is helpful to their children, especially in secondary (87%) as opposed to primary schools (64%). Blazer (2009) suggests that parental involvement in their children's homework can lead to increased companionship as well as greater awareness of what their children are learning in school. There is evidence stemming from this that positive parental attitudes and expectations towards homework can have a positive impact on achievement outcomes (see, for example, Fan & Chen, 2001; Jeynes, 2007, cited in Hallam & Rogers, 2008). However, it is worth pointing out that whereas some pupils express gratitude for this help, others say it can add to their confusion in particularly difficult tasks, especially since parents are not always well versed in the subject knowledge or skills needed. Nonetheless, after reviewing various other studies, Epstein and Van Voorhis (2001) suggested that parental involvement in homework can:

- allow parents to understand what is being taught in class
- facilitate parent-child conversations, which may reinforce the importance of schoolwork
- promote pupils' understanding of how their learning could be used in real-life situations.

See Practitioner Research Box 8.2 for an example of how one of my colleagues put these ideas into practice.

Additionally, effective communication with parents in regard to homework can impact on parent-school relationships, which inevitably support the pupils. For instance, effective communication can:

- allow parents to have a line of communication, or 'connect', with the teachers
- make parents aware and get them involved in curricular activities
- inform parents about how to support their children's school work, especially if parents have to sign planners etc.
- help teachers differentiate for specific learners
- support parents in a way that can help them 'succeed in the role of tutor'
- involve parents in completing assignments, such as through discussion or by answering questions designed by their children.

(Epstein and Van Voorhis, 2001, p. 182)

Practitioner Research Box 8.2
Mike Garvey - To what extent does parental engagement in the development of revision skills improve the outcomes of homework in year 7?

The aims of Mike's Herts & Bucks Challenge Partners' Hub/CamStar research were to implement and evaluate a programme of homework tasks which developed pupils' oracy, subject knowledge and revision skills in year 7 with support from their parents. Essentially, to consolidate their understanding of the topic area and their ability to express themselves at greater length, pupils were asked to teach topics to their parents. The topic area focused on medieval realms in history. Mike used both qualitative and quantitative methods to evaluate the impact of these tasks. Pupils were asked to complete entry and exit surveys, which consisted of multiple-choice and free-text answers.

Mike found that the involvement of parents in homework has a positive effect in terms of pupil confidence around revision skills and of retention of knowledge at least in the short term, especially for boys. This confirms the outcomes of the Teachers Involve Parents in Homework (TIPS) programme, where interactive homework assignments enhanced student writing scores (Epstein et al., 1997). He also found that the high completion rate of pupils in terms of parental signatures indicates that as long as a homework task is light-touch in terms of parental involvement (for example, based on oral feedback) it can be successful. Mike feels that the general trend highlighted by MacBeath and Turner (1990) that 23% of parents never did homework with years 5 and 6 can be changed in the right context. He also believes that his findings confirm the conclusions of Balli (1998) that 95% of pupils responded that their learning often improved when they received help with homework from their parents.

Of course, this research is contextual to the school in question.

Mike is Assistant Headteacher for Teaching and Learning at St. Clement Danes School, Chorleywood, Hertfordshire.

Overzealous parents and homework

It is important to consider how overbearing and controlling parents can negatively impact on their children's achievement (and, of course, wellbeing). Parents who overly structure pupils' homework or are overly critical of it, especially in terms of negative comments, affect pupils' motivation, effort and achievement (Hallam & Rogers, 2018). Vatterott refers to overbearing parents as 'helicopter parents' who hover over the children as they complete homework and who scrutinize every piece of work the children do (2009, p. 34). Moreover, she suggests that pressure from school for pupils to gain good grades can inadvertently affect parents, either causing them to become ever more involved, to the detriment of their children, or causing distress and anxiety. This has led Casanova (1996) to suggest that schools need to be cautious of parents becoming overly involved in the schooling process and of assuming that a lack of visible parental involvement is a sign of uninterest or apathy. As Casanova warns, 'We cannot romanticize parent involvement and proclaim its virtues without also acknowledging its excesses' (Casanova, 1996, p. 31). Therefore, teachers should receive some training that makes them aware of these issues, including how to spot pupil anxiety or distress caused by dominating parents and whom to raise these concerns with if parents need to be contacted. Teachers should also feel confident in either dealing with requests for more homework or knowing whom to ask for support if parents are being unreasonable.

Before we move on, although parental attitudes to homework seem to impact pupils' attitude to it, some question parental involvement on the impact on achievement. Hallam and Rogers (2018), citing various studies, conclude that the evidence is mixed; studies sway between saying parental help improves and impacts achievement to being inconclusive or negligible. On the other hand, Cooper states categorically, '*Yes, it does*' (2007, Chapter 2, Section 6, Paragraph 1). He argues that his meta-analyses suggest that programmes that train parents to get involved in their children's homework have a real impact. Furthermore, he suggests that this is stronger at elementary (primary) school, although there is no data for high schools (secondary schools). This may be so, as other studies suggest that parental involvement is more likely at primary level than secondary level, as pupils are meant to become more autonomous and self-regulated as they progress through school (Hallam & Rogers, 2018).

Key takeaways from Chapter 8

- To properly support pupils, we need to pitch homework at the right ability level for it to be impactful. This is based on not only the findings covered in this subsection but also the views of pupils within The Reach Free School.
- Work that is either too easy or too challenging will be problematic, especially if pupils cannot ask for help from home.
- It is also important that we avoid labelling pupils through too obvious differentiation. Here, it is best that teachers use current ideas and strategies for supporting pupils with learning needs but moderate how obviously this is conveyed to the pupils in question.
- Research shows that pupils also appreciate clubs and online support, which should be encouraged by schools where possible.
- Technology is also useful for setting, facilitating and monitoring homework, but we should also be aware of best practice where possible and the limitations of technology.
- It seems that parental attitudes towards homework do impact children's attitudes towards homework but that parental involvement can have mixed effects. On the one hand, parental involvement can be beneficial if parents genuinely accept that their children need help and have patience with any help they give them. On the other hand, it seems that this involvement can turn sour if parents' expectations are too high. Of course, parents' own knowledge and skills play a part, too. We

need, therefore, to be aware of these limitations so that parents' involvement in their children's work does not do more damage than good. Key here is how we set homework: if pupils find it manageable and doable, parents' help is not necessarily needed.

- It is also evident that schools need clear and concise homework policies, documentation to support parents helping their children with homework and access to the pupils' homework timetables and planners/online homework calendars etc.

Suggested further reading

Hallam, S. & Rogers, L. (2018b). *Homework: The evidence*. London: UCL Institute of Education Press.
As recommended already, this book is extremely authoritative when it comes to reviewing the research on homework, and Chapters 5 and 6 look at pupils' and parents' perspectives on homework respectively. Moreover, Chapter 3 covers various support strategies.
Czerniawski, G. & Kidd, W. (2013b). *Homework for Learning: 300 Practical Strategies*. Maidenhead: Open University Press.
Although I do not recommend all of the strategies or ideas suggested in this book, Chapter 6 suggests strategies for supporting learners, which are certainly useful in most settings, and Chapter 3 looks at differentiation in some depth. However, Chapter 3 does include some ideas that would be questioned by those researchers and writers advocating a more cognitive science-based approach to teaching and learning.

9 Writing a homework policy

Chapter overview

This chapter offers some basic advice on writing policies. It includes how to communicate a policy effectively, legal and statutory requirements in relation to homework policies and Harris Cooper's (1989) views on writing an *evidence-informed* homework policy. The chapter finishes with some examples of homework policies that are in line with the arguments made in this book.

Having a well-written homework policy is the foundation for informing staff, pupils and parents about your school's homework expectations and how this relates to best practice. Ideally, your homework policy, like all policies, will be *research-informed*. Moreover, it is important that you write the policy with your *target audience* – those you want to read the policy – in mind.

Many leaflets produced by government agencies now have the Crystal Mark awarded by the Plain English Campaign. This is to prove that the text is *clear and concise*. Importantly, we should endeavour to make sure all our policies are straightforward so that our target audience understands the aims, procedures and outcomes of the policy in question. Of course, I am not suggesting that schools apply for the Crystal Mark, but the principle of using plain English applies to us as much as anyone else. Additionally, any policy should be *laid out* in a concise way.

Writing a policy

As suggested, ensure that the rationale and objectives of the policy are unambiguous. It is also worth considering subdivisions within the policy to make sure that all key stakeholders, such as teachers, pupils, parents and, if needs be, governors, are included. For example, at The Reach Free School, the Home Learning Policy, which was written in response to the Herts & Bucks Challenge Partners' Hub homework project, has these subdivisions:

- purpose – an explanation of why the policy is needed
- principles – what we are trying to achieve with the policy
- roles of teachers – teachers' roles in achieving the above
- roles of parents, guardians and carers – their roles in achieving the principles
- role of pupils – the pupils' role in achieving the principles
- progression of home learning from year 7 to 13, including the following:
    - years 7, 8 and 9 – a brief summary of our expectations of how much is to be set and how
    - year 10 and 11 – as above
    - post 16 – as above
- monitoring and review – when the policy will be reviewed
- links with other policies – an indication of other policies relevant to this one.

Legal or statutory issues

School policies should indicate that the school complies with legal or statutory guidance. However, homework is different. First, there are no statutory guidelines for homework. As seen in Chapter 7, there used to be guidelines but they were scrapped in 2012. Second, we also know that since 2019 the Office for Standards in Education, Children's Services and Skills (Ofsted) does not include homework in its inspection framework (Ofsted 2019), although I would take that with a pinch of salt. (Essentially, Ofsted could still check that homework is in line with the school's overall teaching and learning policies and strategies, especially if homework is included.) Third, there is no legal requirement for schools to have a homework policy nor have access to it on the website. Nevertheless, it would arguably be poor practice to expect pupils to complete a substantial amount of work away from the classroom and have no easily accessible policy on this.

Communicating the policy

If a homework policy has been written, re-written or significantly changed after a review, then clearly staff need to be informed of how this impacts on their practice. Therefore, training should take place before or around the time the policy comes into force. This can be in an In-Service Education and Training (INSET) session. However, the training should cover the procedures and implementation of the policy. In the case of homework, the expectations for teachers associated with the policy should be modelled as well as explained. Your colleagues should also know where to find the policies to be able to refer to them.

Parents can be informed through email, if necessary, but the policy should be available on the school website and it is also sensible to have paper copies in reception. Although only certain policies are required to be available on the school website (as mentioned above), it makes sense, especially given the advice of Epstein and Van Voorhis (2001) on parental communication (discussed in the previous chapter), that other policies that support staff in communicating teaching and learning issues (including homework) to parents be made accessible online. Staff should be able to email these links to parents if questions are raised about the school's homework policy or practices.

Harris Cooper: homework-specific policies

Cooper (1989a,1989b) reviewed homework policies alongside other documents and suggests that policies should make clear why homework is important, discuss its different purposes, be explicit about expectations in different age groups or phases and clearly explain the role of school administrators and teachers in facilitating this. Cooper does, however, suggest keeping the role of parents to a minimum and avoid suggesting that homework will be overly individualised. Importantly, in relation to the arguments in this book – largely influenced by Cooper's work – he does suggest highlighting the importance of practice tasks within the policy. My own school has considered Cooper's views in formulating our own 'home learning' policy (see Box 9.1).

Examples of homework policies

Below are three examples of homework policies that I feel incorporate the ideas in this book. One example is from a primary school and the other two are from secondary schools. I include sections from the first two examples, but the third – from my own school – is printed in full.

Box 9.1

Reflections from Richard Booth, Headteacher of the Reach Free School, Rickmansworth, on writing homework policies

'Teachers can only deliver so much content to their pupils in the lesson time they have available and therefore a robust homework policy is essential for young people to continue to study away from the classroom. The learning process should be enjoyable and young people should understand the social and economic benefits that this brings. Homework is one important aspect of this, and it should play a part in all schools. In my opinion, the very best homework policies are not overly prescriptive in what they require, but encourage a flexible approach that enables young people to continue learning, studying and building on their knowledge of a particular subject at home'.

Example 9.1

Cranborne Primary School, Potters Bar, Hertfordshire

This policy, written for pupils in Early Years Foundation Stage and Key Stages 1 and 2, does much of what Cooper recommends. For example, the school's rationale for homework is stated in the policy but is referred to as 'our ethos'.

> **Our ethos**: We believe homework can be fundamental to children's progress and attainment. At Cranborne, homework focuses specifically on developing and improving core key skills in English and maths. Homework includes specific activities, set by teachers and supported by parents, to revise skills and consolidate learning.

There are also opportunities for children to develop a real love of learning by engaging in and completing topic-based homework.

The policy also states the types of homework that will be set.

Our expectations:

Early Years Foundation Stage
- *Shared reading with adults at home*
- *Practise reading tricky/red words*
- *Weekly phonics activities*
- *Maths skills tasks*
- *Activities which promote communication*

Key Stage 1 (KS1)
- *Daily reading at home with an adult*
- *Weekly maths skills task*
- *Weekly grammar task*
- *Spelling - year 1 and 2 common exception words*

Lower KS2
- *Reading comprehension task*
- *Weekly maths skills task*
- *Weekly grammar task*
- *Spellings - year 3/4 statutory spelling words*

Upper KS2
- *Reading comprehension task*
- *Weekly maths skills task*
- *Weekly grammar task*
- *Spellings - year 5/6 statutory spelling words.*

The policy gives clear guidelines on the amount of time that homework should take but also indicates that this might not always be the case.

The emphasis is on how homework helps your child to learn rather than on whether it takes a certain amount of time. For example, some children will work quicker than others and get more done in less time. These are the guidelines for primary school children:

- Years 1 and 2: 1 hour per week
- Years 3 and 4: 1.5 hours per week
- Years 5 and 6: 30 minutes per day

Your child shouldn't be expected to spend much longer on homework than the guide times. It doesn't matter if activities don't take as long as the guide times as long as they are useful.

Example 9.2

Cheadle Hulme High School (part of the Laurus Trust), Cheadle Hulme, Cheshire

Cheadle Hulme High School is a mixed comprehensive secondary school in Cheshire. This policy seems to echo Cooper's generic policy in making clear the school's reasons for setting homework as well as the type set. It also makes clear the purpose of homework in that the policy is called a 'Preparation, Practice and Retrieval Policy' as opposed to a 'Homework Policy'. For instance, the policy's 'vision' states:

> In Laurus Trust schools, we refer to homework (work completed by students outside of lesson time) as Preparation, Practice and Retrieval (P,P&R). Teachers set meaningful, relevant work that extends the learning of students within each area of study beyond the allotted curriculum time. The work is linked closely to topics that are being studied and/or builds on core skills that support them in the given subject. Students should feel that P,P&R is both challenging and worthwhile and has a positive effect on progress and attainment whilst fostering a passion for the subject. Students develop the independent study skills and positive learning habits that are essential for success both within the 11–16 school and into further and higher education.
>
> Not all P,P&R is completed at home; for some students who find it hard to work at home or for tasks which require resources more readily available in school, it may be necessary for the P,P&R to be completed at school. Every student is always given this opportunity when required, regardless of background or circumstance. Work set to be completed outside of the classroom will be set as 'preparation', 'practice', or 'preparation and practice'. Subject teachers should make clear to students the type being set and explain how it links it to the learning taking place in class.

It goes on to give examples of preparation and practice tasks and has sections on the amount of homework that will be set as well as how much time should be spent on it. It also includes sections on feedback, which research suggests is vital (see Chapter 6), reasonable adjustments under Equality Act 2010 (including pupils with disabilities) and quality assurance.

Interestingly, the policy states that not all 'PP&R' will be done in school, which mirrors Cooper's view that homework includes all work done outside of instruction time (Bembenutty, 2011).

Example 9.3

The Reach Free School, Rickmansworth, Hertfordshire

Our policy was influenced by the same research that has led to this book. It covers our purpose, principles and expectations of teachers, pupils and, despite Cooper's caution, parents. We have called ours a Home Learning Policy, which is printed in full below.

Home Learning Policy

1. Purpose

    1.1 *Home learning is an invaluable opportunity for pupils to continue their learning outside the timetabled curriculum and is an important element of the achievement aspect of The Reach Free School's ethos. When home learning tasks are set and completed effectively, it becomes a crucial way of raising standards in achievement and encouraging young people to develop a positive attitude to learning that they will carry with them for the rest of their lives.*

    1.2 *Home learning enhances pupils' learning experiences and develops a sense of independence and ownership of their education. Pupils are expected to extend their learning at school by continuing their work at home throughout their years at The Reach Free School.*

    1.3 *Emphasis is placed on the quality and suitability of the learning tasks set. Home learning will be reviewed by subject teachers in accordance with The Reach Free School's Assessment and Marking Policy.*

    1.4 *Pupils will be expected to spend an increasing amount of time on home learning as they progress through the school.*

2. Principles

    2.1 *To encourage pupils to become independent learners, achieve high standards, be creative and acquire personal organisational skills.*

    2.2 *To increase the opportunities for all pupils to reinforce their learning by undertaking tasks at home, which consolidate new knowledge, skills and ideas they have first been introduced to at school or prepare them for learning in later lessons.*

    2.3 *To strengthen the partnership between home and school by giving parents, guardians and carers the opportunity to support and encourage their child's learning in a practical way.*

3. Role of Teachers

    The teaching staff will:

    3.1 *Plan home learning to ensure that it is an integral part of their curriculum planning.*

    3.2 *Set appropriate tasks, based upon the latest available evidence (e.g., practice-based activities and preparation for future learning).*

    3.3 *Set home learning in accordance with Section 6.*

3.4 *Give clearly defined instructions and information needed for the home learning to be completed.*

3.5 *Value pupils' completed work by reviewing it in accordance with The Reach Free School Assessment Policy.*

3.6 *Sanction pupils who do not submit their home learning on the specified day in accordance with The Reach Free School Behaviour Policy.*

3.7 *Ensure that pupils have the appropriate resources required to complete their home learning.*

3.8 *Reward pupils where appropriate for effort, attainment and consistent meeting of deadlines in accordance with The Reach Free School Behaviour Policy.*

4. **Role of Parents, Guardians and Carers**

Parents, guardians and carers are expected to:

4.1 *Provide a reasonably peaceful, suitable place in which pupils can do their home learning - alone or with an adult*

4.2 *Make it clear to pupils that they value home learning and support the school in explaining how it can help their learning*

4.3 *Encourage pupils and praise them when they have completed home learning*

4.4 *Check that children have completed their home learning and fill in the appropriate page in their planners.*

5. **The Role of Pupils**

Pupils are expected to:

5.1 *Actively monitor the homework that has been set for them on Arbor and record when they have submitted it to the teacher*

5.2 *Ask for help if it is not clear to them what they have to do*

5.3 *Approach their home learning with effort, diligence and pride*

5.4 *Submit their home learning on time and in good presentational order.*

6. **Progression of Home Learning from Year 7 to Year 13**

6.1 *Year 7, 8 and 9 - Pupils will be set work for home learning for each subject once a week, allowing, in all subjects other than mathematics, at least two days for it to be completed before the scheduled hand-in day. Owing to the nature of mathematics, it is often expected to be returned the next day. Homework tasks should total around 30 minutes per subject, per week.*

6.2 *Years 10 and 11 - Pupils will be set work for home learning as deemed appropriate by subject teachers, in collaboration with pupils. This will be a minimum of one piece per week per subject, and normal submission deadlines follow at least two days later. Homework tasks should total around one hour per subject, per week.*

6.3 *Post 16 - Pupils will be required to manage their own time and will be issued deadlines within which to complete their work. They will be responsible for their own workload and will be expected to apportion their own time to* complete tasks to or ahead of deadline. Homework tasks should total around three hours per subject, per week.

7. **Monitoring and Review**
   This policy will be monitored and reviewed every two years by The Reach Free School's Governing Body.

8. **Links with Other Policies**
   - *Behaviour Policy*
   - *Special Educational Needs Policy*
   - *Home–School Agreement*

Key takeaways from Chapter 9

- Policies, of all types, need to be clear and concise. Therefore, any homework policy will need to give clear guidance to teachers, pupils and possibly parents of their role in producing homework.
- Ideally, the policy should also specify what types of activities the school expects pupils to complete at home and, if possible, how that impacts on learning.
- Though not a requirement, best practice is to occasionally refer back to homework and the policy in INSET sessions and have this available on your school website.

Suggested further reading

Cooper, H. (1989). Synthesis on Research on Homework. *Educational Leadership*, 47(3) pp. 85–91, especially pp. 89–91.

Though written over 30 years ago, Cooper's advice on writing a generic homework policy seems to chime with the ideas set out in this book, which arguably are based on more recent research. Cooper writes about his views on policies (see box on p. 90) and he gives step-by-step guidance on what a generic policy could include.

Example policies

Cranborne Primary School: https://www.cranborne.herts.sch.uk/learning/home-learning [accessed 30 July 2020]

Cheadle Hulme High School: https://www.laurustrust.co.uk/wp-content/uploads/symlinks/preparation-practice-and-retrieval-policy.pdf [accessed 30 July 2020]

The Reach Free School: https://www.reachfreeschool.co.uk/wp-content/uploads/2019/09/Home-Learning-Policy-V1.3.pdf [accessed 30 July 2020]

10 Final thoughts

At the start of the book, I stated how much I detested homework when at school. For me, it was always a chore – essentially a pointless exercise in domination and control by my teachers. Homework took away my free time to watch television, listen to music or daydream. At home, my parents encouraged me to complete it, which may have added to my rebellious non-compliance as I got older. Nonetheless, perhaps my dreadful performance in my General Certificate of Secondary Education (GCSE) exams – before I went and did everything again at a further education college – is testament to my stubborn refusal not to do anything, my arrogance in knowing better than my well-meaning teachers and concerned parents, my apathetic laziness, or my purposeful forgetfulness. When I think back to those heady days of lethargy, it dawns on me that, with the exception of occasional bravado from friends not wanting to be seen as the teacher's pet or overachieving academically, most of my peers were completing their homework – well, at least some of it anyway. They had fewer detentions, tended to produce something of worth when asked and did better than me in our final exams. When I ask them nowadays, most admit doing it.

Of courses, the above is all anecdotal. However, I did start doing my homework at college where I achieved decent enough A levels to go to university. At university, I found I actually rather enjoyed learning and started taking my studies seriously, even earning the nickname 'Library Boy' from my fellow students. I ended up with a good degree and I have been working hard away from work ever since, which includes writing this book, and I feel this has generally paid off.

Therefore, in terms of moving beyond mere anecdote, I would argue that the evidence we saw in Chapter 2 means we should not give up on homework as a strategy for improving achievement. Yes, the impact is small, but it is there – by and large – in most of the academic studies. This is certainly the case at secondary level and any teacher who ignores this bypasses empirical evidence that has the potential to benefit their pupils.

Subsequently, if we are to set impactful homework, I would point to Chapter 3 and make the case for setting short and concise practice and preparation homework tasks that either build on previous learning – basically consolidating and reinforcing it – or prepare for an upcoming lesson with purposeful and easy-to-access content, such as learning vocabulary, that will be explicitly used in the next lesson or lessons and ideally tested in some low-stakes way. It is important here that pupils see how the homework relates to what they have learnt or are going to learn. I am aware that this is probably self-evident to most readers and not rocket science. Although other types of homework tasks, such as extended project work, can be enriching and rewarding for pupils, I would offer these as optional extras to extend pupils' knowledge if they are intrinsically interested. These types of homework are long and often uneven in terms of parental support, time and even costs. They cannot take precedence, therefore, over ensuring that all pupils have manageable activities that they can realistically and equally participate in.

Practice and preparation tasks also allow us to tap into current best practice in terms of teaching and learning. As seen in Chapters 4, 5 and 6, this can include retrieval practice activities, preparation activities that build on pupils' metacognitive skills and activities that can be tested via low-stakes quizzes once pupils are back in class. There is also no reason why current academic research trends on impactful teaching and learning cannot be harnessed to improve the homework tasks we set. This would include considering how we might apply cognitive load theory, spaced practice and interleaving (discussed in Chapter 7) when setting homework.

Of course, getting people to agree with this will be difficult. Homework is controversial. It always will be. There are also areas that need more investigation or are missing from this book, such as the effect of socioeconomics and the home environment on homework compilation and any impact this has on achievement. Additionally, far more could be said about subject-specific issues, but I am sure that discussion on these could fill separate books solely focused on the various subjects we teach in school. Nevertheless, I feel I have done my homework on this one and felt I should argue the case for homework in this book.

Appendix 1

Understanding the use of effect sizes and correlation coefficients in educational research

Chapter 2 outlined a number of meta-analyses on homework. This appendix seeks to explain how *effect sizes* and *correlation coefficients* measure the impact or the effectiveness of interventions such as homework.

In education, the findings of a meta-analysis often rest on effect sizes, which show whether a teaching strategy or intervention had any impact on achievement. (They can also measure other things, such as attendance, effort or even wellbeing.) Although there are various ways to produce an effect size, researchers generally try to find differences in average results or scores (such as a result or score for those who do homework and those who do not) and divide them by the *standard deviation (d.)*, which tells us how spread out the scores are (basically, the number between the highest and lowest scores). Invariably, researchers calculate the standardised mean difference between the two groups being studied by subtracting the mean of one group from that of the other and then dividing the result by the standard deviation (again, the difference between the highest and lowest scores or result measures) (see Figure A.1).

$$\text{Effect size } (d.) = \frac{\text{[the average mean of one group] - [the average mean of another group]}}{\text{standard deviation}}$$

Figure A.1 A simplified equation for effect sizes

Essentially, in terms of the relationship between a strategy or intervention and achievement, if a group has, on average, increased its scores significantly, the effect size will be more impactful. Moreover, the more the group's scores are spread out, the smaller the effect size will be and the less certain the impact (for a teacher-based explanation, see Weston, 2012). Importantly, an effect size is a very simple measure that gives a rough guide to how impactful a strategy or intervention was.

According to Cohen (1992), effect sizes can be seen to have these effects (or impacts):

- *d.* = 0–0.20 (weak impact)
- *d.* = 0.21–0.50 (modest impact)
- *d.* = 0.51–1.00 (moderate impact)
- *d.* = 1.00+ (strong impact)

Alternatively, according to Cohen, Manion and Morrison (2007), if researchers want to look at the relationship between two variables, such as the amount of time spent on homework and achievement, they can try to measure it using a *correlation coefficient*. Here, researchers can separate effect sizes into five categories on the assumption of the direction of a positive or negative trend (or impact). Correlational techniques are used to answer three questions about two variables or two sets of data: 'First, "Is there a relationship between the two variables (or sets of data)?" If the answer to this question is "Yes", then two other questions follow: "What is the direction of the relationship?" and "What is the magnitude?"' (ibid., p. 531). Therefore, we could see the correlation coefficient (or relationship between variables ($r.$)) as having these correlations or arguably – in the context of this book – impacts:

- $r.$ = 0–0.1 (weak impact)
- $r.$ = 0.2–0.3 (modest impact)
- $r.$ = 0.4–0.5 (moderate impact)
- $r.$ = 0.6–0.8 (strong impact)
- $r.$ = 0.8+ (very strong impact)

A fair number of meta-analyses have been conducted on homework, spanning a broad range of methodologies and levels of specificity as well as using effect sizes based on standard deviation or correlation coefficients. Some of the most significant are compared in Table 2.1 in Chapter 2.

Appendix 2

An analysis of the research into homework types completed by The Reach Free School and Teacher Tapp

The case for practice and preparation over other types: my colleagues' views

Interestingly, my colleagues who researched homework as part of the Herts and Bucks Challenge Partners Hub project largely concur with the research of homework types outlined in Chapter 3. I canvassed their views after they had been looking at their own use of homework and its impact on pupil outcomes throughout the 2017 autumn term. My colleagues were tasked with experimenting with different types of homework assignments over three months. They evaluated the quality of work produced as well as any impact on the pupils' overall understanding of the material taught. Subsequently, over half reported that practice homework tasks were most effective in terms of impact. Of course, we will see that this was not unanimous, but practice homework is clearly perceived as the most useful when compared with the other types discussed in Chapter 3 by the majority (69%) of 16 staff involved in the project (see Figure B.1). Creative and finishing-off homework tasks were considered the least useful by the same staff.

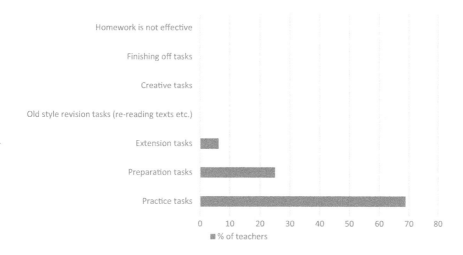

Figure B.1 Teachers' views of which homework tasks have the most impact (as a percentage)

Qualitative staff responses from the Hub and in-school focus group discussions included comments that support their survey choices. For instance, one colleague argued that homework should '[d]evelop the ability of the students to work independently and to practise and apply the skills they have learnt in lessons. It also allows them to see for themselves how good their understanding of a topic is, and therefore to self-evaluate whether they need more help and in which areas'. Similar comments included, 'Homework is set to consolidate and develop the pupils' understanding of the current topic or subject. It should be set in order for the teacher to get an individual view of each pupil's current understanding of the topic or work they are completing'. Some subject-specific comments included, 'Homework in maths is to consolidate classwork. As mentioned in previous sessions, practise is imperative in maths'.

However, not everyone agreed and it needs to be acknowledged that there was no absolute consensus. For example, teachers in English and Spanish felt that preparation (either reading texts or learning new vocabulary) was more impactful. Here, one teacher remarked, 'In Spanish, pupils need to learn vocabulary for the week ahead so lessons can be spent putting their knowledge into practice rather than being taught new words'. Creative arts teachers also felt that homework need not be centred on practice tasks and activities: 'In my opinion homework is different according to each subject area and you can use it in different ways. I think it needs to be targeted and it needs to add to the learning as well as being used to prepare for the lessons. For art, it is important to show progression over time and through setting specific drawing tasks. I give them a menu to choose from that allows for creativity and to address areas that they need to work on'. This teacher felt that extension tasks were important, especially in terms of completing coursework and project work (although creativity and practice in art are arguably symbiotic).

Nonetheless, overall, teachers did agree that practice tasks were essential in the run-up to General Certificates of Secondary Education (GCSEs). They felt that pupils would agree with this, especially in relation to purpose. An analysis of transcripts shows that all teachers agreed that practice tasks should be set regularly – even if built into creative or extension activities – in order to consolidate and reinforce learning. This is evident in this comment from a science teacher: 'The purpose of homework is to consolidate and enhance the learning experience. It should be set when, and only when, it has a clear purpose and is beneficial to that individual pupil'.

Being aware that the Hub schools were secondary, I also contacted colleagues at a nearby primary school. Of the 18 respondents, 78% said that practice was the most impactful type of homework task. Other types were not ruled out entirely, but I think this comment best sums up the views of the teachers surveyed: 'Skills-based rehearsal gives opportunities to develop confidence with material taught in schools. Creative project work is a good way to engage parents with school, but does not suit all families'. Of course, this is a small sample, but the general view of these primary teachers echoes their secondary colleagues.

The case for practice and preparation over other types: Teacher Tapp results

After reviewing the results discussed above, my colleagues completing the Challenge Partners Hub project were interested to know whether teachers elsewhere, and in wider contexts, shared our largely consensual opinions. To answer this, we reached out to Teacher Tapp – an app that sends thousands of teachers questions every day at 3 p.m. – to see if they could help. They did and we had 2,259 more views to help us in our quest to find which homework tasks impact pupils the most.

The results were not too dissimilar to our own. Most (62%) respondents thought that setting homework tasks centred on practising something already taught in class 'best help' pupil outcomes (although they could tick more than one option). This is in agreement with my own colleagues' opinions. Preparation homework was perceived as the second most conducive type of homework task in terms of helping pupils reach their potential (35%). Creative and finishing-off homework activities were seen as the least helpful; this is the same as my school's findings and those of the Hub. Figure B.2 shows the Teacher Tapp findings.

When forced to choose, 40% still chose homework tasks that involve practising previously taught content as the best type of homework activity for helping pupils improve their outcomes in terms of achievement (see Figure B.3).

As Teacher Tapp's Laura McInerney (2018) points out, 'practice varied enormously as a favoured homework type – with a substantial majority (76%) of maths teachers in favour of it, but just over a third of English teachers in favour (35%)'. This is exactly the case with my colleagues; in meetings, my school's maths teachers immediately concurred that practice homework made sense whereas the English teachers argued that preparation homework, especially the reading of texts in advance of lessons, was the most advantageous form of homework. Nonetheless, the English teachers still felt that practice homework activities, particularly those centred on GCSE and A-level questions, were essential preparation for exams. However, primary school and humanities teachers were most likely to opt for extended projects and creative work. Interestingly, creative arts teachers were less likely to pick creative homework tasks than humanities teachers.[1]

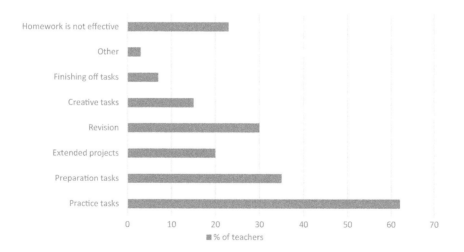

Figure B.2 Teacher Tapp results on which homework tasks have the most impact (as a percentage – respondents could choose more than one task) (adapted from McInerney/ Teacher Tapp, 2018)

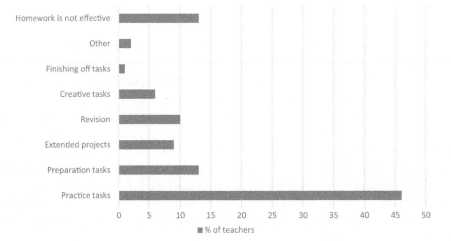

Figure B.3 Teacher Tapp results on which homework tasks have the most impact (as a percentage – respondent's choice limited to one) (adapted from McInerney/Teacher Tapp, 2018)

I was also interested to know whether it is better to set shorter homework tasks for pupils, particularly since the quality of their work away from school may be affected by a lack of concentration because of various distractions, such as social media.

The results also suggest that most teachers understand that setting more than 30 minutes may not be beneficial to pupils.[2] As we saw in Chapter 2, researchers largely concur that the relationship between homework and achievement is curvilinear. In terms of practice, it is arguably important to limit time spent on homework. As also mentioned in Chapter 2, studies have shown that pupils learn more when allowed to practise fewer skills or concepts and that complex processes should be broken down into smaller chunks. Therefore, it can be argued that shorter homework tasks are more conducive for practising skills and allowing for regular practise. Moreover, it can be argued that practice tasks set nightly in some subjects allow for the development of fluency in the application skills. In the long run, these short bursts of practise might be more impactful than hour-a-week homework tasks, especially in subjects like maths and languages. However, this would all need to be coordinated by teachers to make it 'manageable' for pupils.

My pupils' views on the most impactful types of homework

As we very briefly saw in Chapter 8, pupils generally see homework as beneficial. However, many studies suggest that any impact on learning and achievement is dependent on its relevance to things taught and learnt in school. This is why I think many pupils, particularly in secondary school, will begrudgingly accept the relevance and importance of homework if it allows for further practise of the skills learnt in class as well as the application of knowledge via these skills. Of course, in a similar vein, pupils will also see the relevance of preparation homework, which can also be integral to learning in school, so long as its purpose is made explicit and checked or tested in upcoming lessons.

Interestingly, my own pupils concur. In a survey of 50 pupils, 74% said they felt that practice-based homework activities had improved their assessment grades the most. The pupils were asked to complete different types of homework and then qualitatively assess which improved their knowledge, confidence and exam skills, although this was a subjective opinion. They did, however, use their assessed work to make this judgement. The sample consisted of two GCSE religious education classes – one in year 9 and another in year 10 – and lasted for two terms. In the first term, they were set a mixture of homework tasks, including practice (GCSE questions etc.), preparation (reading texts to be studied etc.), creative (making posters etc.) and finishing-off homework. Over a half-term holiday, they were also given longer 'extension' tasks, which involved independent research, and were told simply to 'revise' before assessments (although this task was not included in the first term's survey of pupils' views). Pupils were then asked which type of homework task had the most impact on their learning (see Figure B.4). Although the majority said practice or preparation tasks (37% and 18% respectively), 45% did choose other types. Yes, practice and preparation were deemed the most beneficial, but the results were no knock-out for these over other types.

However, in the second term, pupils were set only practice tasks with the occasional preparation task. Pupils were then asked which homework tasks had the most impact on their learning over the two terms. Here, the results showed that 73% of pupils found practice homework tasks more impactful on learning and achievement than any other type (see Figure B.5). Interestingly, only 6% chose preparation. As already stated, before completing the survey, pupils were asked to review their work over two terms and to compare the quality of their written work alongside their assessment grades (they would have had four formal assessments over this period). The idea was that their views were informed by their progress and achievement and not based on preference.

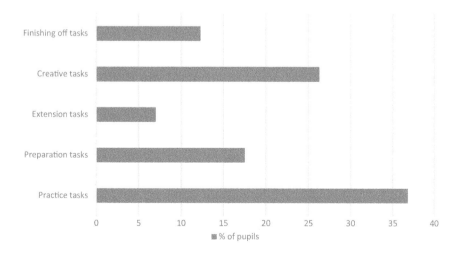

Figure B.4 My pupils' views of which homework tasks have the most impact in term 1 (as a percentage)

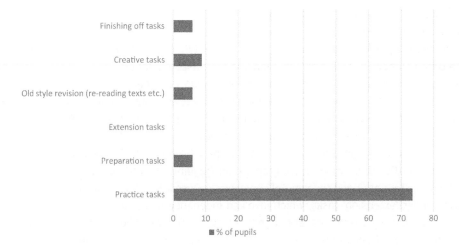

Figure B.5 My pupils' views of which homework tasks have the most impact in term 2 (as a percentage)

Moreover, pupils' actual achievement outcomes also improved over this time. The two classes showed 91% and 92% improvements in attainment (i.e., pupils being on target) over the trial period (where they were set only practice homework tasks) as opposed to 45% and 79% respectively prior to the trial period (where homework tasks were mixed). Of course, claiming this as evidence for the impact of practice or preparation tasks is dubious as other teaching and learning strategies were implemented over this period. Nonetheless, the additional practice, I believed, improved the pupils mastery of knowledge application and fluency of exam skills.

I also sought more qualitative evidence from the pupils through anonymous open-ended questions. Rather than overly analysing these, I will simply let the pupils speak for themselves:

- 'I like it when we get exam questions because it's a really good way to prepare for exams and it helps improve your understanding on the topics'.
- 'Doing past GCSE questions help me because I know what to expect as well as helping me revise and understand the topic more'.
- 'I think that more practice questions work better than the creative homework'.
- 'The type of homework you set is very beneficial to my learning, you have the best type of homework for me out of all my classes'.
- '[I] prefer GCSE questions as that's what you get in the exam'.
- 'Past paper questions with the photocopies of the pages of the textbook to help'.
- 'The surveys to recap and the exam-style questions'.
- 'The questions are very effective'.
- 'I don't enjoy homework, but I think practice GCSE questions will help improve my grades more'.
- 'Exam-style questions about the topic we are doing'.

- '12 markers every other week would be good and maybe something like 4 or 6 markers in between and on half terms an actual exam paper to do'.
- 'I don't really mind. I kinda like homework that helps me in lessons. Also, I do not like too much homework that won't get me anywhere. My fav homework is the GCSE questions and finding things out before the lesson is taught'.

Pupils also commented on the timings of homework tasks, which mirror some of the points made above and in previous chapters, especially in terms of focus and concentration:

- 'I prefer homework that is shorter so then I can do my best at it because I am more focused then on those which are an hour long'.
- 'I absorb more knowledge from shorter homework'.

There were a few outliers to the above:

- 'I personally learn best when I am given the text to read myself – i.e., religious texts, parables etc'.
- 'I find that I remember things more by looking at it and the homework that I like to do are more creative things, so I can remember it easily. I like making slides as well to help remember things as well because I will remember searching up pictures and facts etc'.

It is clear that the pupils in these classes preferred practice homework tasks over any other. I am fully aware that this is a very small and limited study of pupils who will clearly be influenced by my approach to teaching and be tempted to give the answers I am looking for. Nonetheless, I tried to be open-minded and objective in my explanations of homework tasks and I feel that these pupils are completely genuine in their views.

It is worth noting that both groups continued to receive only practice and preparation homework tasks after the trials. In the 2019 summer exams, the year 10 group (then year 11) went on to gain a Progress 8 score of 1.7, which suggested that – on average – pupils gained almost two grades above their estimated grades (these are based on prior attainment data). The group included a high percentage of disadvantaged pupils and English-as-a-foreign-language learners when compared with national averages. The year 9 group went on to attain a Progress 8 score of above 1 in their centre assessed grades in 2020. Therefore, both cohorts were successful and, I feel, my regular setting of practice and occasional preparation homework impacted their achievement and progress scores, which were also significantly higher than the school, county and national averages.

I do understand, however, that some people, including teachers, may see this approach somewhat cynically. The charge of 'teaching to the exam' could be levelled at me, as could the claim that my concentrated setting of practice homework tasks bypasses all the enriching rewards of completing extension tasks or allowing pupils to pursue their own interests. This is something I completely acknowledge and sympathise with. I am also aware that it runs counter to the findings of Joe Carey in Practitioner Research Box 3.2, especially allowing pupils to be 'imaginative' and 'creative' in their homework as well as allowing for choice (see MacBeath & Turner, 1990). Nevertheless, setting regular practice tasks and, if needed, preparation tasks for homework arguably impacts on achievement more than the other types. This, in turn, can improve pupils' achievement in public exams and standardised assessments, which – in the greater scheme of things – impacts more on their overall life chances as they could leave school with a better set of qualifications.

Notes

1 For a full breakdown of the Teacher Tapp findings, see 'What teachers tapped this week - week 42-23 July 2018'. Web. July 28, 2020. Retrieved from: https://teachertapp.co.uk/what-teachers-tapped-this-week-43-23-july-2018/.
2 As above.

Appendix 3

A brief analysis of parent and pupil surveys

What do parents really think?

Many parents echoed the disadvantages listed in Table 1.1 in Chapter 1, giving plenty of arguments against homework.[1] Quite a few focused on its negative impact on family life. For instance: 'It's a major cause of conflict in the home… and I'm a teacher at the school my children attend. Spend my life nagging them, negatives outweigh any benefits'. Others said simply that homework '[c]auses stress and arguments at home'. A few parents mentioned the issues recognised by Professor Peacock in Chapter 3; one parent mentioned, 'I don't feel homework is beneficial overall. It becomes a "whose parent can make the best" with models etc'. There is also the issue of equity here. For instance: 'I find that the parent ends up doing/correcting the work at primary level and so it is not a true reflection on achievement. Children whose parents work all day are at a disadvantage to those with an educated housewife at home who can do work from 3.30 p.m. until 6 p.m. Children with less academic parents are also at a disadvantage as these parents can't help them effectively'. Perhaps the biggest worry was the argument that it takes away free time from children who need to rest, play and enjoy being young. For example, this was a typical response: 'I don't see it achieves anything. Children need a break after learning all day. Evenings and weekends should be family and relaxation time, not time for more pressure and work. Many children are already at after school clubs to accommodate two working parent families. Homework is often done late in the evening, with very little time for focus or care'. Parents also object to being experts in all subjects, as seen in this comment: 'Homework is very stressful in our house… Homework often takes longer than it should, as everything needs explaining and, often, as parents, we have to refresh on modern teaching methods, which have changed considerably since our school days'. Lastly, an argument against homework is that children have less time for extracurricular activities and other things they should do out of school. This sums up that frustration: 'Yes, especially in the shorter days, my son would like to be out on his bike but by the time he has finished his homework it's too late. My daughter would enjoy doing extracurricular clubs but finds when she tries she can't balance her workload'. At the extreme end, there were a few 'I hate it' comments as well as 'it should be banned'!

Despite the overwhelming majority of comments being extremely negative – some sounded rather cross! – it would be disingenuous of me to ignore the positive arguments made by parents. Of course, many saw the academic arguments for homework, such as this response: 'It's a good way to check they've understood and learnt what they've been taught in class'. And this response: 'It's good to reinforce and support learning in school'. These mirror the argument that homework is worthwhile if it relates to learning in school. Similarly, another parent wrote, 'Consolidation is key to effective learning and doing prep for upcoming lessons as homework is great to ensure they are engaged with the subject'. Here, quite a few parents advocated practice and preparation. For example: 'Recall tasks are a must. All evidence shows that only a small percentage of a lesson actually gets retained. Unless we recall it quickly, then mid-term and long-term, it's forgotten'.

Interestingly, many parents argued that homework was relevant only for older pupils. For example, one seemingly positive comment suggested, 'Knowledge retrieval quizzes work best to aid revision for exams. Practice questions are also good. Aside from GCSE [General Certificate of Secondary Education] homework tasks, anything else is pointless'. A fair number of parents clearly argued against homework being set at primary level. This was a common view: 'At KS2 [Key Stage 2] it should be very limited, KS3 should gradually build up', as was this, 'I don't think it's necessary at KS1, should be fun things at KS2 (like make a jelly) and minimal at KS3'. Another argument was that homework should stick to the bare essentials: 'I don't think primary school children should have anything other than reading, spellings and times tables'. Importantly, a number of parents backed up the primacy of reading. For instance: 'No homework at primary school, aside from reading, which remains important'.

Lastly, it was clear that parents of children with special educational needs or learning disabilities were against homework more often than not. One respondent stated, 'My husband is dyslexic and so are 2 of our children. I work long hours. If I'm not at home, it's so stressful for them and it doesn't get done'. Another parent pointed out that '[m]y son has ASD [autism spectrum disorder], homework is something we haven't done since reception (he's now Y3). Endless worksheets causing hour after hour of stress. Not worth it at all'.

What do pupils really think?

Surprisingly, pupils seemed to be a bit more relaxed about homework than their parents (of course, my sample was small and they may have been influenced by the fact that the survey was sent out by me).[2] Quite a lot of them gave positive comments that back up the arguments for homework. For instance: 'It helps us by remembering what we did in the lesson and for extra revision'. This is similar to some of the arguments outlined in Table 1.1 in Chapter 1. Other examples of arguments coming from pupils in defence of homework included, 'It prepares and makes you get better at a certain subject for an upcoming examination or have better knowledge towards a certain subject or topic', as well as, 'I learn a bit in class, but I usually go home and do revision and do the lessons again too. I learn more by myself'. Interestingly, a preference for 'learning by myself' came up a number of times.

It was clear that pupils also appreciated certain types of homework in particular subjects. For instance, a few pupils said things like, 'Reading the next chapter of *Private Peaceful* for English because I got to understand part of the book in my own terms'. Importantly, pre-learning or preparation was mentioned a lot. Pupils said they preferred these tasks. One respondent said they appreciated 'prep homework because you can prepare for an assessment', and another pupil said they appreciated opportunities to '[p]repare for assessments by creating revision pages and mind maps'. In light of the evidence in Chapter 3 on types of homework, pupils also suggested that practice homework tasks are worthwhile. For example, various pupils said things like 'practise questions that come from last year's exams' were helpful and that they found 'practising PEA [point, example and analyse paragraphs] for English [useful] because it helped me gain a solid grasp of PEA'.

However, it goes without saying that some did not look favourably upon homework. The arguments made are similar to those aired by parents, such as encroachment on life outside of school. Typical responses included 'I don't like homework because I get home at 5:20 p.m. and teachers expect me to do homework' and 'I have no time to myself or to spend time with my friends after school'. Another well-aired argument against was homework being set for the sake of it or its repetitiveness. As one pupil explains, 'Generally the homework is just going over what we learned in lessons with a few exceptions, meaning it's boring and uninspiring'. Some pupils objected to disjointed assignments: 'We get quite a lot, especially in some subjects, when teachers just give you out of the blue homework expecting it due for tomorrow'. There were also arguments against in recognition that parents might have been taught differently. For example: 'I don't think that homework helps us because if we are stuck on something we might ask someone else at home and they might tell us a different way to do it and that will make us more confused than we already were so it will be more work for the teacher and students'. Too much homework was another regular complaint. For instance: 'Sometimes I find it hard to complete the work on time because although the homework might be set for 30 mins it might take me an hour'. Lastly, the practicality of resourcing homework was raised as a bone of contention, which is a concern raised by parents and also recognised by Professor Peacock earlier. As one pupil put it, 'Making something, because u don't have the time or maybe even equipment to do that. I walk to school for 18 mins, how am I supposed to get it to school, if it's raining or windy'.

Conclusions

Although this is an unscientific *vox pop* of sorts, it is clear that the common arguments for and against homework are evident here. Arguments for homework tend to focus on the academic benefits of additional opportunities to practice and extend knowledge outside of the classroom or as a way to better prepare for upcoming lessons. The limits of curriculum time and homework's potential to alleviate some of the scarcity of learning time were also cited, as was the idea that homework develops other skills, such as independence and self-regulation.

However, there are clearly common arguments against homework too. Some parents worry that they do not have the skills to support their children, and many deplore the perceived attack on children's leisure time, as do many pupils. For many parents, in particular, it is evident that homework can create friction at home as the pressures to complete work and parents' need to support teachers hit the boiling point with their reluctant and often exhausted children. Having to do poorly set homework tasks was another gripe, as was the relevance of these tasks to pupils' overall learning.

Nevertheless, quite a few pupils – not cited above – said they prefer small-sized homework tasks. It could well be that homework has an important role to play in their overall education but that it is not always well set, nor relevant nor conducive to a home/life balance. Perhaps, then, it does need reconceptualising or at least streamlining.

Notes

1 I used Facebook, Twitter and LinkedIn for this survey and gained 64 anonymous responses.
2 This survey included 29 pupils from The Reach Free School and was anonymous. Pupils were selected from all year groups and did not focus on any particular subject. Questions were open, not closed. The survey is separate from the pupil survey in Chapter 4, which is discussed in Appendix 2.

Bibliography

Ambuehl, H. J. (1941). *A survey of parent teacher and pupil attitudes regarding homework*. University of Southern California. Retrieved from: https://search-proquest-com.ezproxy.herts.ac.uk/docview/1621285531?accountid=14660 [accessed 1 June 2020].

Anderson, L. W., Krathwohl, D. R., Airasian, P. W., Cruikshank, K. A., Mayer, R., Pintrich, P. R., Raths, J. & Wittrock, M. C. (2001). *A taxonomy for learning, teaching, and assessing: a revision of bloom's taxonomy of educational objectives*. New York, NY: Longman.

Azmitia, M. & Cooper, C. R. (2001). Good or bad? Peer influences on latino and european american adolescents' pathways through school. *Journal of Education for Students Placed at Risk (JESPAR)*, 6 (1-2), 45-71.

Bain, K. (2004). *What the best college professors do?* Cambridge, MA: Harvard University Press.

Baker, R. (2007). *The perspectives of pupils, parents and teachers, in a secondary school, regarding the role of homework*. PhD Thesis, University of Hull.

Balli, S. J. (1998). When mom and dad help: Student reflections on parent involvement with homework. *Journal of Research and Development in Education*, 31(3), 142-148.

Balli, S. J., Demo, D. H. & Wedman, J. F. (1998). Family involvement with children's homework: An intervention in the middle grades. *Family Relations: An Interdisciplinary Journal of Applied Family Studies*, 47(2), 149-157.

Baş, G., Şentürk, C. & Ciğerci, F. M. (2017). Homework and academic achievement: A meta-analytic review of research. *Issues in Educational Research*, 27(1), 31-50.

Bembenutty, H. (2011). The last word: An interview with Harris Cooper - Research, policies, tips, and current perspectives on homework. *Journal of Advanced Academics*, 22(2), 340-350.

Bempechat, J. (2004). The motivational benefits of homework: A social-cognitive perspective. *Theory Into Practice*, 43(3), 189-196.

Beyer, B. K. (1987). *Practical strategies for the teaching of thinking*. Boston, MA: Allyn and Bacon.

Birnbaum, M., Kornell, N., Bjork, E. & Bjork, R. (2012). Why interleaving enhances inductive learning: The roles of discrimination and retrieval. *Memory and Cognition*, 41(3), 392-402.

Bjork, R. (n.d.). *Applying cognitive psychology to enhance educational practice*. Retrieved from: https://bjorklab.psych.ucla.edu/research/ [accessed 9 May 2020].

Bjork, R. A. (1994). Memory and metamemory considerations in the training of human beings. In J. Metcalfe & A. P. Shimamura (Eds.), *Metacognition: Knowing about knowing*, 185-205. Cambridge, MA: The MIT Press.

Bjork, E. L. & Bjork, R. A. (2011). Making things hard on yourself, but in a good way: Creating desirable difficulties to enhance learning. In M. A. Gernsbacher, R. W. Pew, L. M. Hough, J. R. Pomerantz (Eds.) & FABBS Foundation, *Psychology and the real world: Essays illustrating fundamental contributions to society*, 56-64. New York, NY: Worth Publishers.

Bjork, R. A. & Bjork, E. L. (2019a). Forgetting as the friend of learning: Implications for teaching and self-regulated learning. *Advances in Physiology Education*, 43(2), 164-167.

Bjork, R. A. & Bjork, E. L. (2019b). The myth that blocking one's study or practice by topic or skill enhances learning. In C. Barton (Ed.), *Education myths: An evidence-informed guide for teachers*. Woodbridge, UK: John Catt Educational Ltd, pp. 57-70.

Black, P. (1990). Homework: The sixth day of instruction. *ERS Spectrum, 8*(2), 35–41.

Black, P. & Wiliam, D. (2001). *Inside the black box: Raising standards through classroom assessment.* Retrieved from: http://weaeducation.typepad.co.uk/files/blackbox-1.pdf [accessed 18 July 2020].

Blazer, C. (2009). *Homework literature review.* Miami, FL: Miami-Dade County Public Schools Research Services.

Bloom, B. S. (1956). *Taxonomy of educational objectives, handbook: The cognitive domain.* New York, NY: David McKay.

Brooks, J. G. & Brooks, M. G. (2001). Becoming a constructivist teacher. In: A. L. Costa (Ed.), *Developing minds: a resource book for teaching thinking,* 150–157. Alexandria, VA: Association for Supervision and Curriculum Development.

Bromley, M. (2017, January 18). Teaching practice: Explanations and modelling, *SecEd.* Retrieved from: https://www.sec-ed.co.uk/best-practice/teaching-practice-explanations-and-modelling/ [accessed 10 June 2020].

Brown, P. C., Roediger, H. L., III & McDaniel, M. A. (2014). *Make it stick: The science of successful learning.* Cambridge, MA: The Belknap Press of Harvard University Press.

Buell, J. (2004). *Closing the book on homework: Enhancing public education and freeing family time.* Philadelphia, PA: Temple University Press.

Buijs, M. & Admiraal, W. (2013). Homework assignments to enhance student engagement in secondary education. *European Journal of Psychology of Education, 28*(3), 767–779.

Carpenter, S. K. (2014). Spacing and interleaving of study and practice. In V. A. Benassi, C. E. Overson & C. M. Hakala (Eds.), *Applying science of learning in education: Infusing psychological science into the curriculum,* 131–141. Washington, DC, WA: Society for the Teaching of Psychology.

Carpenter, S. K. & Agarwal, P. K. (2019). *How to use spaced retrieval practice to boost learning.* Ames, IA: Iowa State University.

Carpenter, S. K., Cepeda, N. J., Rohrer, D., Kang, S. H. K. & Pashler, H. (2012). Using spacing to enhance diverse forms of learning: Review of recent research and implications for instruction. *Educational Psychology Review, 24*(3), 369–378.

Carr, N. S. (2013). Increasing the effectiveness of homework for all learners in the inclusive classroom. *School Community Journal, 23*(1), 169–182.

Casanova, U. (1996). Parent involvement: A call for prudence. *Educational Researcher, 25*(8), 30–46.

Cepeda, N. J., Vul, E., Rohrer, D., Wixted, J. T. & Pashler, H. (2008). Spacing effects in learning: A temporal ridgeline of optimal retention. *Psychological Science, 19*(11), 1095–1102.

Christodoulou, D. (2013). *Seven myths of about education.* Abingdon: Routledge.

Coe, R. (2019, December 5). *EEF blog: Does research on 'retrieval practice' translate into classroom practice?* Retrieved from: https://educationendowmentfoundation.org.uk/news/does-research-on-retrieval-practice-translate-into-classroom-practice/ [accessed 8 June 2020].

Coe, R., Aloisi, C., Higgins, S. & Major, L. E. (2014). *What makes great teaching? Review of the underpinning research. Project Report.* London: Sutton Trust.

Cohen, J. (1992). Statistical power analysis. *Current Directions in Psychological Science, 1*(3), 98–101.

Cohen, L., Manion, L. & Morrison, K. (2004). *A guide to teaching practice.* London: Routledge.

Cohen, L., Manion, L. & Morrison, K. (2007). *Research methods in education* (6th ed.). Abingdon: Routledge.

Cooper, H. (1989a). *Homework.* White Plains, NY: Longman.

Cooper, H. (1989b). Synthesis of research on homework. *Educational Leadership, 47*(3), 85–91.

Cooper, H. (2007). *The battle over homework: common ground for administrators, teachers, and parents.* Thousand Oaks, CA: Corwin Press.

Cooper, H., Jackson, K., Nye, B., & Lindsay, J.J. (2001). A model of homework's influence on the performance evaluations of elementary students. *Journal of Experimental Education, 69*(2), 181–189.

Cooper, H. Lindsay, J.J., Nye, B. & Greathouse, S. (1998). Relationships among attitudes about homework, amount of homework assigned and completed, and student achievement. *Journal of Educational Psychology, 90*(1), 70–83.

Cooper, H., Robinson, J. C. & Patall, E. A. (2006). Does homework improve academic achievement? A synthesis of research, 1987–2003. *Review of Educational Research, 76*(1), 1–62.

Cooper, H. & Valentine, J. C. (2001). Using research to answer practical questions about homework. *Educational Psychologist, 36*(3), 143–153.

Corno, L. (1996). Homework is a complicated thing. *Educational Researcher*, *25*(8), 27–30.

Cotton, K. (2001). *Classroom Questioning*. New Jersey: Office of educational Research and Improvement/North West Regional Educational Laboratory.

Coughlan, S. (2013, January 6). Gove sets out 'core knowledge' curriculum plans. *BBC news*. Retrieved from: https://www.bbc.co.uk/news/education-21346812 [accessed 19 June 2020].

Cowan, R. & Hallam, S. (1999). *What do we know about homework?* London: Institute of Education, University of London.

Czerniawski, G. & Kidd, W. (2013). *Homework for learning: 300 practical strategies*. Maidenhead: Open University Press/McGraw-Hill Education.

Dai, J. (2016). An empirical study on the influence of mobile media on college students' autonomous learning in the "internet +" era. *Heilongjiang Higher Education Research*, (8), 132–136.

Danielson, M. L., Storm, B. & Kramer, K. (2011). Real homework tasks: A pilot study of types, values, and resource requirements. *Educational Research Quarterly*, *34*(5), 17–32.

Darling-Hammond, L. & Ifill-Lynch, O. (2006). If they'd only do their work! *Educational Leadership*, *63*(5), 8–13.

Dean, G. (2016). *Teacher knowledge of grammar in the primary school*. PhD thesis, University of Exeter.

DeVries, R. & Kohlberg, L. (1990). *Constructivist early education: Overview and comparison with other programs*. Washington, DC, WA: National Association for the Education of Children.

Didau, D. (2016). *What if everything you knew about education was wrong?* Carmarthen: Crown House Publishing.

Didau, D. & Rose, N. (2016). *What Every Teacher Needs to Know about … Psychology*. Woodbridge, UK: John Catt Educational Ltd.

DfE (2013). *Teachers' standards: guidance for school leaders, school staff and governing bodies*. London: DfE.

DfE (2014). *Statutory guidance: National curriculum in England: English programmes of study*. DfE: London. Retrieved from: https://www.gov.uk/government/publications/national-curriculum-in-england-english-programmes-of-study/national-curriculum-in-england-english-programmes-of-study [accessed 9 June 2020].

DfE (2016). *Eliminating unnecessary workload around marking: Report of the independent teacher workload review group*. Retrieved from: https://assets.publishing.service.gov.uk/government/uploads/system/uploads/attachment_data/file/511256/Eliminating-unnecessary-workload-around-marking.pdf [accessed 1 August 2020].

DfE (2017). 'Importance of core knowledge sees return of textbook': Transcript of speech given by Nick Gibb at Policy Exchange, London, 30 November 2017. Retrieved from: https://www.gov.uk/government/speeches/nick-gibb-importance-of-core-knowledge-sees-return-of-textbooks [accessed 9 June 2020].

DfE (2019). *Key stage 4 performance (revised)*. DfE: London. Retrieved from: https://www.gov.uk/government/statistics/key-stage-4-performance-2019-revised [accessed 1 June 2020].

DfEE (1998). *Homework: guidelines for primary and secondary schools*. London: DfEE.

Dobozy, E. (2010). *Homework: Its forms and functions revisited. Proceedings of Catholic Education Office Curriculum Conference*. Perth,Catholic Education Office.

Doherty, J. (2017). Skilful questioning: The beating heart of good pedagogy. *Impact - Journal of the chartered college of teaching*. Retrieved from: https://impact.chartered.college/article/doherty-skilful-questioning-beating-heart-pedagogy/ [accessed 18 May 2020].

Dorking, M. C. (2019, September 2). Ofsted cuts homework checks from inspection: Should children have to study outside of school? *Yahoo news*. Retrieved from: https://uk.style.yahoo.com/ofsted-homework-cuts-children-banned-112153876.html [accessed 29 May 2020].

Duncan, A. (2010). Teachers' views on dynamically linked multiple representations, pedagogical practices and students' understanding of mathematics using TI-Nspire in Scottish secondary schools. *ZDM - International Journal on Mathematics Education*, *42*(7), 763–774.

Dunlosky, J. (2013). Strengthening the student toolbox. *American Educator*, *37*(3), 12–21.

Dunlosky, J., Rawson, K. A., Marsh, E. J., Nathan, M. J. & Willingham, D. T. (2013). Improving students' learning with effective learning techniques: Promising directions from cognitive and educational psychology. *Psychological Science in the Public Interest*, *14*(1), 4–58.

Edwards, W. (2017) *'What is the point of homework and should schools set it?'* EdD thesis, University of Bedfordshire.

EEF (2020a). *Educational endowment foundation teaching and learning toolkit: Homework primary.* Retrieved from: https://educationendowmentfoundation.org.uk/evidence-summaries/teaching-learning-toolkit/homework-primary/ [accessed 16 April 2020].

EEF (2020b). *Educational endowment foundation teaching and learning toolkit: Homework secondary.* Retrieved from: https://educationendowmentfoundation.org.uk/evidence-summaries/teaching-learning-toolkit/homework-secondary/ [accessed 16 April 2020].

EEF (2018). *Metacognition and self-regulated learning: Guidance report.* Retrieved from: https://educationendowmentfoundation.org.uk/public/files/Publications/Metacognition/EEF_Metacognition_and_self-regulated_learning.pdf [accessed 27 June 2020].

Elder, L. & Paul, R. (2002). *The miniature guide to the art of asking essential questions.* Santa Rosa, CA: Foundation for Critical Thinking.

Epstein, J. L. (1998). *Interactive homework: Effective strategies to connect home and school.* Paper presented at *The annual meeting of the American Educational Research Association*, San Diego, CA.

Epstein, M. H., Polloway, E. A., Foley, R. M. & Patton, J. R. (1993). Homework: A comparison of teachers' and parents' perceptions of the problems experienced by students identified as having behavioral disorders, learning disabilities, or no disabilities. *RASE: Remedial & Special Education, 14*(5), 40–50.

Epstein, J. L., Simon, B. S. & Salinas, K. C. (1997). Involving parents in homework in the middle grades. *Research Bulletin, 18,* 1–4.

Epstein, J. L. & Van Voorhis, F. L. (2001). More than minutes: Teachers' roles in designing homework. *Educational Psychologist, 36*(3), 181–193.

Eren, O. & Henderson, D. J. (2011). Are we wasting our children's time by giving them more homework? *Economics of Education Review, 30*(5), 950–961.

Ericsson, A. K. (2008). Deliberate practice and acquisition of expert performance: A general overview. *Academic Emergency Medicine, 15*(11), 988–994.

Esner, M. (2017, October 10). Making a fuss about whole-clas feedback. Retrieved from: https://teachreal.wordpress.com/2017/10/10/making-a-fuss-of-feedback/ [accessed 5 August 2020].

Fan, X. & Chen, M. (2001). Parental involvement and students' academic achievement: A meta-analysis. *Educational Psychology Review, 13*(1), 1–22.

Fan, H., Xu, J., Cai, Z., He, J. & Fan, X. (2017). Homework and students' achievement in math and science: A 30-year meta-analysis, 1986–2015. *Educational Research Review, 20,* 35–54.

Firth, J. (2018). The application of spacing and interleaving approaches in the classroom. *Impact - Journal of the chartered college of teaching* [online]. Retrieved from: https://impact.chartered.college/article/firth-spacing-interleaving-classroom/ [accessed 29 June 2020].

Fitts, P. M. & Posner, M. I. (1967). *Human performance.* Belmont, CA: Brooks/Cole.

Fraser, B. J., Walberg, H. J., Welch, W. W. & Hattie, J. A. (1987). Syntheses of educational productivity research. *International Journal of Educational Research, 11*(2), 147–252.

Galloway, M., Conner, J. & Pope, D. (2013). Nonacademic effects of homework in privileged, high-performing high schools. *The Journal of Experimental Education, 81*(4), 490–510.

Galton, M. (2002). Continuity and Progression in Science Teaching at Key Stages 2 and 3. *Cambridge Journal of Education, 32* (2), 250–265.

Gove, M. (2013, February 6). *Ofqual policy steer letter: Reforming Key Stage 4 qualifications.* Retrieved from: https://assets.publishing.service.gov.uk/government/uploads/system/uploads/attachment_data/file/529404/2013-02-07-letter-from-michael-gove-reform-of-ks4-qualifications.pdf [accessed 7 June 2020].

Graue, M. E., Weinstein, T. & Walberg, H. J. (1983). School-based home instruction and learning: A quantitative synthesis. *The Journal of Educational Research, 76*(6), 351–360.

Hallam, S. (2004, February 9). 'Pupils' perspectives on homework. *The guardian.* Retrieved from: https://www.theguardian.com/education/2004/feb/09/schools.uk [accessed 9 April 2020]

Hallam, S. (2006). *Homework: its uses and abuses.* London: Institute of Education, University of London.

Hallam, S. & Rogers, L. (2018). *Homework: the evidence.* London: UCL Institute of Education Press.

Hargreaves, D. H., Hester, S. & Mellor, F. J. (1975). *Deviance in classrooms.* London: Routledge & Kegan Paul.

Harris, D., & Williams, J. (2012). The association of classroom interactions, year group and social class. *British Educational Research Journal, 38*(3), 373–397.

Hartjes, L. B. (2011). *Homework completion rates and student self-perception of homework ability in secondary students with disabilities.* Masters dissertation, Southwest Minnesota State University.

Hattie, J. A. (1992). Measuring the effects of schooling. *Australian Journal of Education*, 36(1), 5-13.

Hattie, J. (2009). *Visible learning: A synthesis of over 800 meta-analyses relating to achievement.* London: Routledge.

Hattie, J. & Yates, G. C. R. (2014). *Visible learning and the science of how we learn.* London: Routledge.

Haydn, T. (2013). First do no harm: Assessment, pupil motivation and learning. In S. K. Capel, M. Leask & Turner, T. (Eds.), *Learning to teach in the secondary school*, 417-438. London: Routledge.

Healy, M. J. R. (1990). Measuring importance. *Statistics in Medicine*, 9(6), 633-637.

Hill, C. (1994). Testing and assessment: An applied linguistic perspective. *Educational Assessment*, 2(3), 179-212.

Hodkinson, A. & Smith, C. (2018). Chronology and the new national curriculum for history: Is it time to refocus the debate? *Education, 3-13, 46*(6), 700-711.

Holmes, M. & Croll, P. (1989). Time spent on homework and academic achievement. *Educational Research*, 31(1), 36-45.

Hoover-Dempsey, K. V., Battiato, A. C., Walker, J. M., Reed, R. P., DeLong, J. M. & Jones, K. P. (2001). Parent involvement in homework. *Educational Psychologist*, 36(3), 195-209.

Hong, E., Mason, E., Peng, Y. & Lee, N. (2015). Effects of homework motivation and worry anxiety on homework achievement in mathematics and English. *Educational Research and Evaluation*, 21(7-8), 491-514.

Hong, E., Peng, Y. & Rowell, L. L. (2009). Homework self-regulation: Grade, gender, and achievement level differences. *Learning and Individual Differences*, 19(2), 269-276.

Howard, E. & Khan, A. (2019). *GCSE reform in schools: The impact of GCSE reforms on students' preparedness for A level maths and English literature.* Coventry: Ofqual.

Jackson, D. (2014). *Geeks, boffins, swots and nerds: a social constructionist analysis of 'gifted and talented' identities in post-16 education.* Doctoral thesis, UCL Institute of Education.

Jackson, N. (2004). Developing the concept of metalearning. *Innovations in Education and Teaching International*, 41(4), 391-403.

Jensen, E. (2008). *Brain-based learning: The new paradigm of teaching.* Thousand Oaks, CA: Corwin Press.

Jeynes, W. H. (2007). The relationship between parental involvement and urban secondary school student academic achievement: A meta-analysis. *Urban Education*, 42(1), 82-110.

Jones, A. B. (2017). *Teaching Sociology Successfully.* London: Routledge.

Jones, A. B. (2019a, March 1). Convince me homework is worth doing. *TES.* Retrieved from: https://www.tes.com/magazine/article/convince-me-homework-worth-doing [accessed 29 April 2020].

Jones, A. B. & Essery, M. (2018). Q: How can we reduce teacher workload without affecting the quality of marking? A: Whole-class feedback. *My college: Windows into the classroom - Chartered college of teaching.* Retrieved from: https://my.chartered.college.temp.link/2018/10/how-reduce-teacher-workload-quality-marking-whole-class-feedback/ [accessed 10 May 2020].

Jones, K. (2019b). *Retrieval practice: Research & resources for every classroom: Resources and research for every classroom.* Woodbridge, UK: John Catt Publications Ltd.

Karpicke, J. D. (2012). Retrieval-based learning: Active retrieval promotes meaningful learning. *Current Directions in Psychological Science*, 21(3), 157-163.

Karpicke, J. D. & Bauernschmidt, A. (2011). Spaced retrieval: Absolute spacing enhances learning regardless of relative spacing. *Journal of Experimental Psychology: Learning, Memory, and Cognition*, 37(5), 1250-1257.

Katz, I., Kaplan, A. & Gueta, G. (2009). Students' needs, teachers' support, and motivation for doing homework: A cross-sectional study. *The Journal of Experimental Education*, 78(2), 246-267.

Keys, W., Harris, S. & Fernandes, C. (1997). *Third international mathematics and science study, second national report. Part 2: Patterns of mathematics and science teaching in upper primary schools in England and eight other countries.* Slough: National Foundation for Educational Research.

Kirby, J. (2015, May 3). A 5 year revision plan. *Joe Kirby's blog.* Retrieved from: https://pragmaticreform.wordpress.com/2015/05/03/a-5-year-revision-plan/ [accessed 6 June 2020].

Kohn, A. (2006). *The homework myth: Why our kids get too much of a bad thing.* Cambridge, MA: Da Capo Press.

Kohn, A. (2012, Spring). The truth about homework. *Pathways to family wellness magazine.* (33). Retrieved from: http://pathwaysofamilywellness.org/component/option,com_crossjoomlaarticlemanager/Itemid,/aid,2248/view,crossjoomlaarticlemanager/ [accessed 19 April 2018].

Lage, M., Platt, G. & Treglia, M. (2000). Inverting the classroom: A gateway to creating an inclusive learning environment. *Journal of Economic Education, 31*(1), 30–43.

Lam, J. W. (1996). *The employment activity of chinese-american high school students and its relationship to academic achievement*. Master's Thesis. Arlington, TX: University of Texas.

Lee, J. F. & Pruitt, K. W. (1979). Homework assignments: Class games or teaching tool? *Clearing House,* 53(1), 31–35.

Lee, Y. & Kinzie, M. B. (2012). Teacher question and student response with regard to cognition and language use. *Instructional Science: An International Journal of the Learning Sciences, 40*(6), 857–874.

Lemov, D. (2015). *Teach like a champion 2.0: 62 techniques that put students on the path to college*. San Francisco, CA: Jossey-Bass.

Leven, T. & Long, R. (1981). *Effective instruction*. Washington, DC: Association for Supervision and Curriculum Development.

Li, Y. (2018). Current problems with the prerequisites for flipped classroom teaching - a case study in a university in Northwest China. *Smart Learning Environments, 5*(2). Retrieved from: https://doi.org/10.1186/s40561-018-0051-4 [accessed 19 May 2020].

Lo, C. K. & Hew, K. F. (2017). A critical review of flipped classroom challenges in K-12 education: Possible solutions and recommendations for future research. *RPTEL,* 12(4). Retrieved from: http://doi.org10.1186/s12909-018-1144-z [accessed 19 May 2020].

MacBeath, J. & Turner, M. (1990). *Learning out of school: Homework, policy and practice. A research study commissioned by the Scottish Education Department*. Glasgow: Jordanhill College.

Marzano, R. J. (2005). Homework and practice. Retrieved from: https://escmarzano.wikispaces.com/4+Homework+and+Practice [accessed 9 February 2018].

Marzano, R. J. (2017). *The new art and science of teaching*. Bloomington, IN: Solution Tree Press.

Marzano, R. J. & Pickering, D. J. (2007). The case for and against homework. *Educational Leadership,* 64(6), 74–79.

Marzano, R. J., Pickering, D. & Pollock, J. E. (2001). *Classroom instruction that works: Research-based strategies for increasing student achievement*. Alexandria, VA: Association for Supervision and Curriculum Development (ASCD).

Maudsley, D. B. (1979). *A theory of meta-learning and principles of facilitation: An organismic perspective*. Toronto: University of Toronto.

Mazur, E. (1997). *Peer instruction: A user's manual series in educational innovation*. Upper Saddle River, NJ: Prentice Hall.

Mazur, A., Brown, B. & Jacobsen, M. (2015). Learning designs using flipped classroom instruction/ Conception d'apprentissage à l'aide de l'instruction en classe inversée. *Canadian Journal of Learning and Technology/La revue canadienne de l'apprentissage et de la technologie, 41*(2). Retrieved from: https://doi.org/10.21432/T2PG7P [accessed 7 May 2020].

McDermott, K. B. & Roediger, H. L. (2020). Memory (encoding, storage, retrieval). In R. Biswas-Diener & E. Diener (Eds.), *Noba textbook series: Psychology*. Champaign, IL: DEF publishers. Retrived from: http://noba.to.bdc4uger [accessed 29 April 2020].

McInerney, L. (2018). What teachers tapped this week. *Teacher tapp blog*. Retrieved from: http://teachertapp.co.uk/2018/07/what-teachers-tapped-this-week-43-23-july-2018/ [accessed 28 July 2018].

McLeod, S. A. (2013). *'Stages of memory - encoding storage and retrieval,' Simply psychology*. Retrieved from: https://www.simplypsychology.org/memory.html [accessed 6 June 2020].

McPherson, F. (2005). Homework - is it worth it? Retrieved from: http://www.mempowered.com/children/homework [accessed 29 May 2020].

Melton, A. W. (1963). Implications of short-term memory for a general theory of memory. *Journal of Verbal Learning and Verbal Behavior, 2*(1), 1–21.

Meyer, B., Haywood, N., Sachdev, D. & Faraday, S. (2008). *Independent learning: Literature review* (Research Rep. No. DCSF-RR051). London: Learning and Skills Network.

Mezirow, J. (1981). *A critical theory of adult learning and education. Adult Education, 32*(1), 3–24.

Mikk, J. (2006). *Students' homework and TIMSS 2003 mathematics results*. Paper presented at the *International Conference on Teaching Mathematics: Retrospectives and Perspectives*, Tartu, Estonia.

Minke, T. A., (2017). Types of homework and their effect on student achievement. *Culminating projects in teacher development*. 24. Retrieved from: https://repository.stcloudstate.edu/ed_etds/24 [accessed 10 September 2018].

MIT Open Learning (n.d.). *Spaced and interleaved practice*. Retrieved from: https://openlearning.mit.edu/ mit-faculty/research-based-learning-findings/spaced-and-interleaved-practice [accessed 9 August 2020].

Muhlenbruck, L., Cooper, H., Nye, B. & Lindsay, J. J. (1999). Homework and achievement: Explaining the different strengths of relation at the elementary and secondary school levels. *Social Psychology of Education: An International Journal*, 3(4), 295-317.

Mullis, I. V. S., Martin, M. O. & Foy, P. (2016). *TIMSS 2015 international results in mathematics*. Chestnut Hill, MA: TIMSS & PIRLS International Study Center, Boston College.

Murillo, F. & Martínez-Garrido, C. (2012). Homework influence on academic performance. A study of Iberoamerican students of primary education/Incidencia de las tareas para casa en el rendimiento académico. *Un estudio con estudiantes iberoamericanos de Educación Primaria. Revista de Psicodidáctica*, 18(1). Retrieved from: https://ojs.ehu.eus/index.php/psicodidactica/article/view/6156 [accessed 12 August 2020].

Murre, J. M. J. & Dros, J. (2015) Replication and analysis of Ebbinghaus' forgetting curve. *PLoS One*, 10(7), e0120644.

Neilson, W. 2005. Homework and performance for time-constrained students. *Economics Bulletin*, 9(1), 1-6.

Nelson, J. S., Epstein, M. H., Bursuck, W. D., Jayanthi, M. & Sawyer, V. (1998). The preferences of middle school students for homework adaptations made by general education teachers. *Learning Disabilities Research & Practice*, 13(2), 109-117.

Newell, A. & Rosenbloom, P. S. (1981). Mechanisms of skill acquisition and the law of practice. In J. R. Anderson (Ed.), *Cognitive skills and their acquisition*, 1-55. Hillsdale, NJ: Lawrence Erlbaum Associates.

Newmark, B. (2018, August 1). Nothing new, just a review part 2. *Ben newmark blog*. Retrieved from: https://bennewmark.wordpress.com/2018/08/01/nothing-new-just-a-review-part-2-from-good-to-great-how-to-improve-retrieval-practice/ [accessed 26 April 2020].

November, A. & Mull, B. (2012). Flipped learning: a response to five common criticisms. *November Learning*. Retrieved from: http://novemberlearning.com/assets/flipped-learning-a-response-to-five-common-criticisms.pdf.

Núñez, J. C., Suárez, N., Rosário, P., Vallejo, G., Cerezo, R. & Valle, A. (2015). Teachers' feedback on homework, homework-related behaviors, and academic achievement. *The Journal of Educational Research*, 108(3), 204-216.

OECD (2014). Does homework perpetuate inequities in education? *PISA in focus*, No. 46, Paris: OECD Publishing.

Ofsted (2017). *Ofsted's blog: What parents told us about homework*. Retrieved from: https://www.tes.com/blog/ofsteds-blog-what-parents-told-us-about-homework [accessed 24 June 2020].

Ofsted (2019). *School inspection handbook*. London: DfE.

Pan, S. (2015, August 4). The interleaving effect - mixing it up boosts learning. *Scientific American*. Retrieved from: https://www.scientificamerican.com/article/the-interleaving-effect-mixing-it-up-boosts-learning/ [accessed 6 May 2020].

Pan, S., Pashler, H., Potter, Z. & Rickard, T. (2015). Testing enhances learning across a range of episodic memory abilities. *Journal of Memory and Language*, 83, 53-61.

Paschal, R. A., Weinstein, T. & Walberg, H. J. (1984). The effects of homework on learning: A quantitative synthesis. *The Journal of Educational Research*, 78(2), 97-104.

Patall, E. A., Cooper, H. & Robinson, J. C. (2008). Parent involvement in homework: A research synthesis. *Review of Educational Research*, 78(4), 1039-1101.

Payne, R. (2015). Using rewards and sanctions in the classroom: Pupils' perceptions of their own responses to current behaviour management strategies. *Educational Review*, 67(4), 483-504.

Perry, J., Lundie, D. & Golder, G. (2019). Metacognition in schools: What does the literature suggest about the effectiveness of teaching metacognition in schools? *Educational Review*, 71(4), 483-500.

Peterson, E. & Irving, S. (2008). Secondary school students' conceptions of assessment and feedback. *Learning and Instruction*, 18, 238-250.

Pickering, D. (2003). *Research-based strategies for increasing student achievement*. Paper presented at *The Virginia Association for Supervision and Curriculum Development Conference*, Williamsburg, Virginia.

Prensky, M. (2001). Digital natives, digital immigrants part 1. *On the Horizon*, 9(5), 1-6.

Quigley, A. (2012). Top ten questioning strategies. *The confident teacher blog*. Retrieved from: https://www.theconfidentteacher.com/2012/11/questioning-top-ten-strategies/ [accessed 5 May 2020].

Rau, M. A., Aleven, V. & Rummel, N. (2010). Blocked versus interleaved practice with multiple representations in an intelligent tutoring system for fractions. In V. Aleven, J. Kay & J. Mostow (Eds.), *Intelligent tutoring systems*. ITS 2010. Lecture Notes in Computer Science, vol. 6094. Berlin: Springer.

Roediger, H. L. (2013). Applying cognitive psychology to education: Translational educational science. *Psychological Science in the Public Interest, 14*(1), 1–3.

Roediger, H. L. & Karpicke, J. D. (2006). Test-enhanced learning: Taking memory tests improves long-term retention. *Psychological Science, 17*(3), 249–255.

Roediger, H. L., Putnam, A. L. & Smith, M. A. (2011). Ten benefits of testing and their applications to educational practice. In J. P. Mestre & B. H. Ross (Eds.), *The psychology of learning and motivation: Vol. 55. The psychology of learning and motivation: Cognition in education*, 1–36. Cambridge, MA: Elsevier Academic Press.

Rohrer, D. (2012). Interleaving helps students distinguish among similar concepts. *Educational Psychology Review, 24*(3), 355–367.

Rohrer, D., Dedrick, R., Hartwig, M. K. & Cheung, C. (2019). A randomized controlled trial of interleaved mathematics practice. *Journal of Educational Psychology, 112*, 40–52.

Rohrer, D., Dedrick, R. F. & Stershic, S. (2015). Interleaved practice improves mathematics learning. *Journal of Educational Psychology, 107*(3), 900–908.

Rosadi, A. (2017). The effectiveness of anagram technique in teaching vocabulary. *Voices of English Language Education Society, 1*(1).

Rosário, P., Núñez, J. C., Vallejo, G., Cunha, J., Nunes, T., Mourão, R. & Pinto, R. (2015). Does homework design matter? The role of homework's purpose in student mathematics achievement. *Contemporary Educational Psychology, 43*, 10–24.

Rose, N. (2017, September 8). Why punishments and rewards don't work. *TES online*. Retrieved from: https://www.tes.com/magazine/article/why-punishments-and-rewards-dont-work [accessed 2 August 2020].

Rosenshine, B., (2012). Principles of instruction: Research-based strategies that all teachers should know. *American Educator, 36*(1), 12–19.

Rowe, M. B. (1986). Wait time: Slowing down may be a way of speeding up! *Journal of Teacher Education, 37*(1), 43–50.

Sammons, Pam, Sylva, Kathy, Melhuish, Edward, Siraj, Iram, Taggart, Brenda, Toth, Katalin & Smees, Rebecca. (2014). *Influences on students' GCSE attainment and progress at age 16: Effective pre-school, primary & secondary education project (EPPSE)*. London: DfE Research Brief.

Samson, G. K., Strykowski, B., Weinstein, T. & Walberg, H. J. (1987): The effects of teacher questioning levels on student achievement. *The Journal of Educational Research, 80*(5), 290–295.

Savery, J. R. (2006). Overview of problem-based learning: Definitions and distinctions. *Interdisciplinary Journal of Problem-Based Learning, 1*(1), 9–20.

Schmidt, R. A. & Bjork, R. A. (1992). New conceptualizations of practice: Common principles in three paradigms suggest new concepts for training. *Psychological Science, 3*(4), 207–217.

Sealy, C. (2019). Memorable experiences are the best way to help children remember. In N. Barton (Ed.), *The researchEd guide to education myths*. Woodbridge, UK: John Catt Publications, pp. 29–40.

Seng, S. H., Tey, S. H. & Fam, A. (1993). *Metacognition and metalearning essential differences*. Paper from the *ERA Conference*, Singapore, 23–25 September 1993. Retrieved from: https://repository.nie.edu.sg/bitstream/10497/15461/1/ERAS-1993-SengASH.pdf [accessed 2 August 2020].

Sharpe, C., Keys, W. & Benefield, P. (2001). *Homework: A review of research*. Slough: NFER.

Shatz, I. (n.d.). Interleaving: How mixed practice can boost learning. *Effectiviology*. Retrieved from: https://effectiviology.com/interleaving/ [accessed 6 August 2020].

Shea, J. B. & Morgan, R. L. (1979). 'Contextual interference effects on the acquisition, retention, and transfer of a motor skill'. *Journal of Experimental Psychology: Human Learning and Memory, 5*(2), 179–187.

Shellard, E. G. & Turner, J. R. (2004). *ERS focus on…Homework: Research and best practice*. Arlington, VA: Educational Research Service.

Sherrington, T. (2012). Homework: What does the Hattie research actually say? *TeachHead blog*. Retrieved from: https://teacherhead.com/2012/10/21/homework-what-does-the-hattie-research-actually-say/ [accessed 29 May 2020].

SMF (2013). 'The Progressive Betrayal': Transcript of speech delivered at the Social Market Foundation by Michael Gove, Secretary of State for Education, London, 5 February 2013. Retrieved from: http://www.smf.co.uk/michael-gove-speaks-at-the-smf/ [accessed 9 June 2020].

Solomon, Y., Warin, J. & Lewis, C. (2002). Helping with homework? Homework as a site of tension for parents and teenagers. *British Educational Research Journal*, 28(4), 603–622.

Stahl, R. J. (1990). Using "think-time" behaviors to promote students' information processing, learning, and on-task participation. *ERIC clearinghouse for social studies/social science education*. Retrieved from: https://www.ericdigests.org/1995-1/think.htm [accessed 18 May 2020].

Strandberg, M. (2013). Homework – is there a connection with classroom assessment? A review from Sweden. *Educational Research*, 55(4), 325–346.

Suárez, N., Regueiro, B., Epstein, J. L., Piñeiro, I., Díaz, S. M. & Valle, A. (2016). Homework involvement and academic achievement of native and immigrant students. *Frontiers in Psychology*, 7, 1517.

Tofade, T. S., Elsner, J. L. & Haines, S. T. (2013). Best practice strategies for effective use of questions as a teaching tool. *American Journal of Pharmaceutical Education*, 77(7), 155.

Trautwein, U. & Köller, O. (2003). The relationship between homework and achievement–still much of a mystery. *Educational Psychology Review*, 15(2), 115–145.

Trautwein, U., Lüdtke, O., Schnyder, I. & Niggli, A. (2006). Predicting homework effort: Support for a domain-specific, multilevel homework model. *Journal of Educational Psychology*, 98(2), 438–456.

Tymms, P. B. & Fitz-Gibbon, C. T. (1992). The relationship of homework to A-level results. *Educational Research*, 34(1), 3–10.

Vatterott, C. (2009). *Rethinking homework: Best practices that support diverse needs*. Alexandria, Va: ASCD.

Vukman, K. B. & Licardo, M. (2010). How cognitive, metacognitive, motivational and emotional self-regulation influence school performance in adolescence and early adulthood. *Educational Studies*, 36(3), 259–268.

Walberg, H. J. (1999). Productive teaching. In H. C. Waxman & H. J. Walberg (Eds.), *New directions for teaching practice and research*. Berkeley, CA: McCutchen Publishing Corporation, pp. 75–104.

Walberg, H. J. & Paik, S. J. (2000). *Effective educational practices. Educational practices series 3*. Paper presented at *The International Academy of Education*, Brussels (Belgium).

Wang, C. (2009). The impact of new media on the life, study and thinking of college students. *Theoretical Front of Universities*, 07, 40–41.

Waters, J., Kupski, S. & Craven, S. (2013). Cross-curricular homework: how does it impact on attainment, engagement and teaching?. In A. Riggall, R. Churches & A. Elwick (Eds.), *Action research for school improvement Studies on able, gifted and talented learners, homework and white working-class pupils*, 21–28. Reading: CBfT.

Watson, A. (2018, August 30). Grammar and creativity in the English national curriculum. *BERA blog*. Retrieved from: https://www.bera.ac.uk/blog/grammar-and-creativity-in-the-english-national-curriculum [accessed 27 April 2020].

Weston, D. (2012, November 26). When is an effect size inefficient? *Teacher development trust blog*. Retrieved from: https://tdtrust.org/when-is-an-effect-size-ineffective [accessed 26 November 2018].

Willingham, D. (2006, Spring). How knowledge helps: It speeds and strengthens reading comprehension, learning–And thinking. *American educator*. Retrieved from: https://www.aft.org/periodical/american-educator/spring-2006/how-knowledge-helps [accessed 5 May 2020].

Witzel, B. S. & Mercer, C. D. (2003). Using rewards to teach students with disabilities: Implications for motivation. *Remedial and Special Education*, 24(2), 88–96.

Woolfolk, A., Hughes, M., & Walkup, V. (2008). *Psychology in education*. Harlow: Pearson.

Xu, J. (2006). Gender and homework management reported by high school students. *Educational Psychology*, 26(1), 73–91.

Xu, J. & Corno, L. (1998). Case studies of families doing third-grade homework. *Teachers College Record*, 100(2), 402–436.

Yu, Y. (2015). *The influence of types of homework on opportunity to learn and students' mathematics achievement: Examples from the university of chicago school mathematics project*. PhD thesis University of South Florida.

Index

Page numbers in *italics* refer to figure; Page numbers in **bold** refer to table.

Ingram Content Group UK Ltd.
Milton Keynes UK
UKHW050648150623
423413UK00022B/75

9 780367 637446